How About Keeping Fish

by

Val Singleton

and

Dick Mills

ep

EP Publishing Limited

Acknowledgements

The publishers would like to thank the following for allowing their photographs to be reproduced in this book:

Heather Angel — cover, pp. 19, 20, 28, 32, 61 (2), 70 (2), 73, 74, 75, 76, 78 (2), 80 (2), 81, 82, 83 (2), 84, 85
Chris Beever — frontispiece
Bruce Coleman Ltd (photographs by Jane Burton and Hans Reinhard) — pp. 8, 27, 29, 32, 77, 79
Dr David Ford — p. 14
Dick Mills — pp. 38, 40, 53
Bernard Pye — pp. 61, 62 (2)

The publishers would also like to thank the following for their help: Aquarian Advisory Service, Keith Barraclough, Laurence G. Perkins, Karen Roberts.

The layout and artwork are by Chris Beever

ISBN 0 7158 0659 9
Published by EP Publishing Ltd, East Ardsley, Wakefield, West Yorkshire, 1979

The Authors

Valerie Singleton trained as an actress at the Royal Academy of Dramatic Art before becoming one of the main presenters of 'Blue Peter', the most successful British children's programme. From 'Blue Peter' she moved on to 'Tonight', the news digest at peak viewing time.

Dick Mills has been keeping fish for nearly twenty years, and is a council member of the Federation of British Aquatic Societies for whom he produces a quarterly magazine. He also lectures on the hobby and has contributed many articles to the aquatic press. He says that the hobby is a complete relaxation from his more noisy job of making special sound sequences for BBC TV programmes like Dr Who!

Contents

The Types of Fishkeeping

The first experience most people have of keeping fish comes from winning a goldfish in a funfair or at a local fête. Unfortunately many of these goldfish die quickly and their owners are deterred from making another attempt. It is worth persevering, however, because keeping fish is a fascinating and absorbing hobby. The reason for the goldfish's death was probably that its container was inadequate. There is just not enough space in the typical small round bowl, and filling the bowl to the brim with water does nothing to improve matters: insufficient oxygen is let in from the surface of the water and so the fish suffocates.

Funnily enough, goldfish are the fish that are least suitable to be kept indoors and do best in a garden pond where they can grow really large. However, goldfish represent just one branch of the hobby, the one called coldwater fishkeeping. Other coldwater fish are the sticklebacks and minnows that you can find in streams. The most popular branch of the hobby comprises the tropical freshwater fish of which there are so many different varieties available. Most of this book is devoted to this kind of fishkeeping. Lastly you could consider marine aquaria, keeping sea fish (tropical or coldwater) and other sea-creatures. As marine fishkeeping poses a number of additional problems it is not really suitable for the beginner.

The Chinese were keeping and breeding goldfish for decorative purposes two thousand years ago, but it was not until comparatively recently that interest in fishkeeping, particularly tropical species, became really widespread in the West. The centre of the new hobby was Germany, from where aquarium fishes were exported to America. The hobby in Britain was also gaining momentum, and one of our modern-day aquatic magazines was founded as long ago as 1924; however, the 1939-45 war interrupted the growing enthusiasm which fortunately picked up again in the late 1940s. Ironically enough, a spin-off from the war years may have contributed most to the future development of the hobby. Jet travel has made it possible to transport quickly to our shops fish that have been caught on the other side of the world, so there are now several hundred different species imported into this country. One of the most enjoyable by-products of becoming a keen aquarist is that because

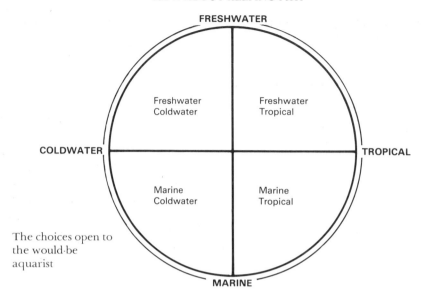

FRESHWATER

Freshwater
Coldwater

Freshwater
Tropical

COLDWATER

TROPICAL

Marine
Coldwater

Marine
Tropical

MARINE

The choices open to
the would-be
aquarist

The outmoded, inadequate goldfish bowl

8

the hobby is so popular internationally you can make friends with people in other countries, sharing with them your fishkeeping experiences. It is not only letters that can be exchanged — sometimes you can even swap fish eggs.

I have several friends who keep aquariums and have aways loved watching the fish swimming leisurely around; but I wanted to find out more about the hobby from a real expert, so I went off one morning to meet Dick Mills. Dick has been keeping fish for nearly twenty years and has become very involved in the hobby; in addition to belonging to his local aquarist Society he is also a Council Member of the Federation of British Aquatic Societies for whom he produces a quarterly magazine. On top of this he also visits other aquarist societies giving lectures and has contributed many articles to the aquatic press. He enjoys the hobby immensely and says it is a complete contrast to and relaxation from his more noisy job of making special sound sequences for BBC TV programmes like Dr Who!

An Easy Hobby

I asked Dick first of all how he came to take up the hobby. He replied that he won his first aquarium as a reward for passing his eleven plus exam. A visit to London and he had become the proud owner of a tank, three gold-fish and, of course, all the bits and pieces that go in the tank and make it look so pretty: gravel, rocks and plants. Sadly, Dick lost interest, and a year later the goldfish were growing bigger in an uncle's pond and the tank had gone rusty! But as Dick said himself, the aquatic seeds had been sown and when he was older they began to sprout, so that now he has a fascinating collection of fish and quite a number of tanks. There may be only one aquarium in his sitting room, but when I visited his garden shed I was amazed at how many tanks he housed in such a small space. It showed that even the tiniest flat has room for at least one aquarium.

It looked to me as though the hobby could be expensive and time-consuming, but Dick told me that it was quite the opposite: once the initial outlay has been made on setting up the tank, the fish are fairly inexpensive and easy to look after. They only need a few minutes' attention each day and perhaps a couple of hours at the weekend. Unlike other pets fish never leave fur or hairs around the house — they don't ask to be walked late at night either! Even holidays present few problems. The fish can be left quite happily unattended for a week or two, and this means that virtually anyone can participate in the hobby. Of course, as in all hobbies or pastimes, it can become an obsession and a few newcomers always try to do everything at once. This is fine for those that can afford it, but it is a little off-putting for the rest of us! One good thing about fish-keeping is that no special clothing is required as would be obligatory in a sporting hobby (although it you are going off to a local pond to catch some live food for your fish, a pair of 'wellies' might be advisable). It is also a clean, comfortable hobby and in these days of 'environmental-awareness' fishkeeping may be regarded as a conservation-orientated interest.

The most striking thing about Dick's fish was how attractive they were. Most of them were highly coloured, and they come in all sorts of shapes and sizes, from the minute mosquito fish whose males are barely an inch long to the stately angel fish that can measure five or six inches in depth.

I quickly saw how the different types of fish behaved in different ways — some gathering in small shoals, others swimming alone; some probing at the bottom of the tank, others feeding near the surface. This variety among the different species is one reason why an aquarist's potential for enjoyment is unlimited: there is so much to learn about the hobby. Eventually fishkeepers go on to breed their fish, and here there is yet more scope for the hobby to be rewarding and fun.

How should you first learn something about this pastime? Well the best way is to go and see as many aquariums as you can. You may know people who already keep fish; but if you don't it doesn't matter because you can always go into a pet shop or tropical fish shop and look at the aquariums there. Talk to the people who run the shops and ask their advice. Another excellent thing to look out for is a fish show; these are frequently held by local societies and anyone can go along and give them-selves an idea of the range of the hobby and which fish they like the look of most. The idea of a fish show may seem quite odd to you but I'm sure that you are already quite familiar with other 'animal' shows for dogs, cats, rabbits, cagebirds, etc. Fish shows are just the same (although a lot quieter!). Owners bring along their pets for judges to assess, and the trophies to be won are just as coveted as those sought after by other pet owners. In addition to shows organised by local societies, there are a number of major shows around Britain sponsored by magazines and manufacturers, and organised by national or area bodies. Strangely enough a public aquarium or zoo is not the best place to visit as not all the exhibits are fish likely to be kept in the home aquarium. All the same, they are interesting places to spend an afternoon and often give lots of information about fish, their habits and history. When I was in America

'Not all the zoo exhibits are fish likely to be kept in the home aquarium'!

recently I spent a whole day at Boston in the most exciting aquarium I have ever seen. I learnt a lot about fish that previously I never even knew existed!

Another valuable source of information is books. On page 94 Dick gives a list of the ones he thinks you will find most useful, and the majority of these should be obtainable from your local library. It is a good idea to read several (by different authors) to get a balanced view. Some of the inform-ation you will need — such as how to set up a tank, the reasons for plants and which fish you can put together — will be found in the following pages of this book. You will also need more detailed knowledge about fish illness and signs that a tank is not operating properly.

Your First Tank

How much money you spend when you first start depends on you, but a tank two feet long, twelve inches deep and fifteen inches high with the lamps, thermostatically controlled heater, fish and plants will probably cost about £25 to £30. It is wise to go to a reputable dealer who will, as I have just said, most likely give you some help and advice. For various reasons you will need a cover to go over the tank. This will stop the dust getting in, keep your cat, if you have one, from being a little too inquisitive, hold the light bulbs and retain the heat. Fish can also jump quite a bit, and so another use of the cover is to curb those exuberant leaps for freedom.

Light is important in a tank. It helps the plants to grow and it enables your fish to see; it also allows you to see them. Nobody wants an unlit tank of fish they can't see as a feature in their sitting room — hardly a colourful addition to the décor! In their natural surroundings fish are accustomed to light coming from above them. If you put your fish tank in a window so the only source of light strikes the side of the tank you will soon find your fish tilting their bodies over and presenting their backs to the light. This means they would appear to be swimming on their sides! How much light you put in your tank is critical and greatly affects the balance of your tank. If your tank is at the back of a dark room it will not receive enough light. On the other hand, if it is on a windowsill there might well be too much and, as I have just said, the light would be coming in from the wrong angle.

Sunlight alone is far too variable, although it can be used as a supplementary source of light. It is most important that the lighting should be arranged so that you can regulate and control it. Remember, fish do actually sleep and rest even if they have no eyelids, so they must have at least eight hours of darkness. The best time for this is is when you are sleeping too. If you have to go away for any length of time it is possible to buy a time clock for your lights. If you are only away for a week or two you can switch the lights off because a short period without light will not harm your fish.

As I have said fishkeeping is divided into three quite distinct areas — coldwater fish, tropical fish and marine fish. Coldwater fish include our native fish and the fancy goldfish varieties. These can all be kept in unheated aquariums although you might find the native fish more difficult to look after than goldfish. Marine fish include those found around our shores and those from tropical reefs of the Pacific and Indian Oceans. These fish are the newcomers to the hobby and it is only in recent years that people have been able to keep them successfully.

'Tropical' fish are the freshwater fish that come from tropical parts of the world and that most people keep in their aquariums. As they tend to be smaller than goldfish you can keep more of them together in a tank, which is one reason for their popularity. In the wild they live in water which is rather warmer than that found in our own streams and lakes, so your aquarium water has to be heated a little, usually to about 72 — 75°F, depending on the type of fish. This temperature is really only lukewarm; I think you would still find the water a little cold for swimming. I have said that the temperature is 'usually' 72 — 75°F, but remember that this will

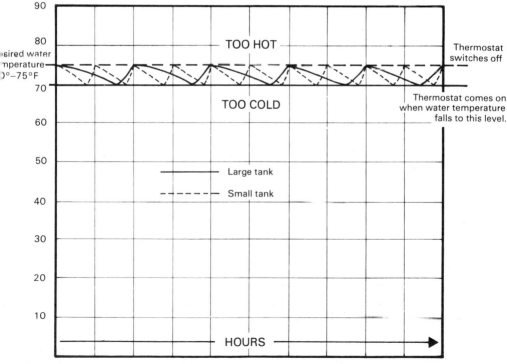

How a thermostat operates

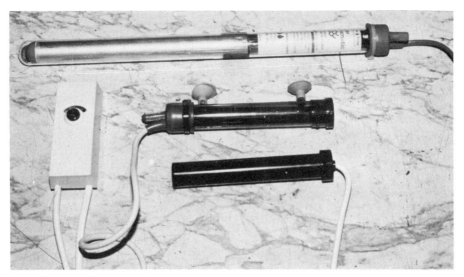

A small range of heaters and thermostats

not be suitable for all the different species of fish you can buy. This is another reason for learning as much as possible before you start.

The heater is controlled by a *'thermostat'*, an ingenious device that turns the heater off when the water reaches the required heat. Then turns the heater on again when the water cools to a predetermined temperature. The same principle is used in central heating and (in reverse) in your refrigerator. Aquarium heaters use some electricity, but really cost very little to run.

Besides a wide range of fish, Dick's aquariums also contained many sorts of attractive plants, some of which were rooted, some floating. Plants certainly make an aquarium prettier and more 'natural' looking, but that is by no means their only use. Although oxygen is absorbed through the surface of the water, plants also help to provide it, in the process removing some of the waste matter in the tank. How this is done is shown in the diagram opposite. Fish like to have plants for another reason — they provide shade, shelter and security, just as in the fishes' natural rivers and lakes where they must often hide from larger predators. For similar reasons plants are necessary when fish are breeding: fish eggs and young fish 'fry' are often eaten by the adult fish unless they are hidden by bushy plants. Some fish seek the leaves of plants as places to lay their eggs. Lastly, many fish are vegetarian and appreciate plants as food — so don't be surprised if your plants get smaller or disappear altogether!

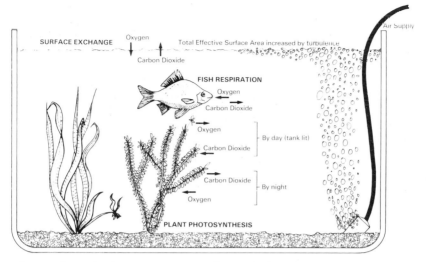

How plants and aeration improve gaseous exchanges in the aquarium

Many aquarists find the plants almost as fascinating as the fish. This is particularly true on the Continent where aquascaping talents have to be seen to be believed! Dick enjoys taking cuttings from his plants and growing his own to furnish new tanks. If you like gardening you would know about this already; if not it is yet another interesting side line of fishkeeping to explore.

It is also fun to landscape your tank with some rocks, and this is fine as long as you are careful to use smooth stones that cannot cut and damage fish. Also to be avoided are rocks such as limestone, or those that contain mineral ore; these can upset the chemical composition of the water. Some care must be taken to place the rocks so that fish cannot become trapped between them.

One of the aggravations of fishkeeping is a form of plant life known as 'algae', a slimy green moss that feeds on nutrients in the same way as other plants and can grow over everything rather like weeds taking over a flowerbed. At the same time this algae is one of the indicators you can use to see if you have got your tank's 'balance' right. This balance is obtained when the fish and plants live together in the water in harmony so that the fish are lively, the plants thrive and the tank looks clean and pleasant. When you achieve this the tank will almost run itself. A certain amount of light green algae can indicate that all is well; for instance it is a sign that the water is not too acid, as it might be if no algae could live. Again, algae needs some light to grow, so if there are just a few patches on the rocks or glass near the source of light, your lighting is probably correct; but if the same green algae grows rather rapidly this is a sign that you have too much light. Too little light is indicated by brownish looking algae. A darker brown algae as well as a bluish and dark green shades usually indicate either an excess of light or else too much unconsumed food in the water. All this sounds terribly complicated and technical to me, but Dick gave me another tip as a method of controlling the spread of algae — plant *more* plants. Again like flowerbed technology, if you give the weeds (algae) less room in which to grow, or provide more competition for the light that is available, then they won't get a start in your tank!

A *short* suck is all that's needed when syphoning. To clean up the gravel the tube should be lower in the tank

16

Once you have got the 'balance' right you can keep a tank for years without too much management apart from the occasional bit of clearing up. It is likely that the bottom of the tank will get covered with dead leaves that have fallen off plants, and it is a good thing to syphon these out and to change the water partially about once a month or fortnight. This will go a long way towards keeping down unwanted matter in your tank. Syphoning is very easy once you master the knack. You can have lots of sophisticated attachments to your tank like mechanical filtration but it is just as simple to syphon off with a length of hose. Dip one end into the tank and suck at the other end. You will soon get the hang of stopping just before you get a mouthful of muddy aquarium water! Then put the end into a bucket and take off as much as you need to change the water or to remove any rubbish. Remember when you top the water up to make sure it is close to the temperature of the water already in your tank; it will upset your fish if you unexpectedly add lots of cold.

From page 54 onwards Dick explains in some detail how to go about choosing your first tank and equipment, and how to set the tank up. One mistake I would have made would have been to have gone and bought fish straight away in my impatience to get started. When you think about it, it makes sense to put the aquarium in its permanent place, fill it with water, plants and rocks, fit the heating and lighting, and then leave the whole lot for a couple of weeks. This gives the plants chance to establish themselves and it also gives you time to see that the lighting and heating are correct.

Choosing Fish

While your tank is settling down you can come to a final decision about which fish you are going to buy, bearing in mind the following points:
- Some fish are more expensive than others.
- Some fish are easier to keep than others.
- The fish you buy will most likely grow, so you must allow for this and buy fewer fish at the start.
- Large fish sometimes eat small fish, so be careful which species you mix.
- Some fish like to swim in shoals and should not be bought singly or in pairs.
- The males of some fish will fight if put in an aquarium together.
- Different fish like to be at different levels in the tank, so you can spread your population evenly through the water.

The fish that are easiest to keep are the livebearing species and the colourful barbs and tetras which Dick describes from page 72 onwards. It would be a good idea to start off with these — they are pretty and active, are stocked by most fish shops and are not expensive. Gradually, as you learn more about the different species, you can move on to the more difficult fish. In his section of this book Dick also gives a guide as to which fish are surface swimmers, and those which feed on the bottom or in the middle of the tank. In general you can recognise the top feeders by their protruding and upturned mouths, evolved in this way because in their natural surroundings they feed off insects that are on the water surface. Fish in the middle range of water come in all shapes and sizes, from miniature torpedoes to the disc-like angel fish which are most at home slipping between reeds.

On the very bottom of the tank are the fish that grub around scavenging, among them the loaches and catfish. Although they are not brilliantly coloured, I particularly like catfish; they are amusing, entertaining fish with downturned mouths and the whiskers that give them their name. In fact these whiskers are quite sensitive and if the gravel is too sharp they may become worn down and have to grow again. Some aquarists recommend keeping catfish simply because they help to keep a tank clean. Dick is very much against this and believes that you should

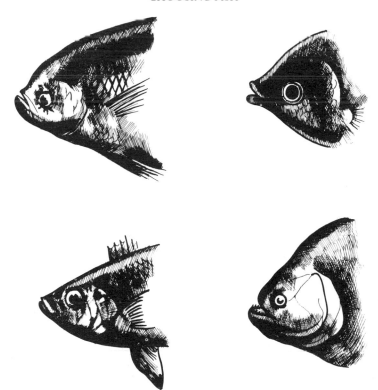

Some hungry mouths: *(top left)* midwater feeder; *(top right)* algae browser; *(bottom left)* surface feeder; *(bottom right)* meat-eater

A bottom-feeding tropical Catfish

Note the large eyes of this baby Black Shark *(Mornlius chrysophekadion),* an indication that it will grow greatly in size — in this case from 2—3 inches up to 20 inches long!

keep a species of fish only if you like it, not just because it is useful. There are many families of catfish, the most common ones — armoured catfish — coming from South America. Other families come from Africa, among them a type which swims upside down!

Among the points I suggested you bear in mind when you choose your fish is the fact that they will grow in size. Actually it is hard to determine how much they will grow — puppies give an indication of future growth by the size of their feet, but fish have no such feature apart, perhaps, from the eyes. Fishes with large eyes may very well turn out to be large fish when adult, on the other hand they may have large eyes in order to see with in their natural, wild habitat which is probably very muddy water. It may come as a shock to them when they find themselves in your nice clean clear-water tank! Another point to consider — and the dealer should tell you things like this — is that some fishes change quite a lot between youth and adulthood; in addition to colour changes, their character may take a turn for the worse, and that very attractively marked young fish might well end up being a drab, overbearing bully of your aquarium. This is where a look around fish shows comes in handy. Most of the fishes in the show will be of adult size, so if you choose your fishes from this selection you won't go far wrong. Although you will find it hard to judge the age of your new fish, most of those sold in shops will have been obtained from foreign breeders when they are two or three months old. In this case you can be fairly certain that the fish will double in size.

When you get to the shop and start to select your fish it is important to choose those that look to be healthy. You might wonder how on earth you can tell when a fish looks fit. Well, healthy fish sparkle well, they seem alert, their fins will be a little more displayed, they will look glossy and have a more intense colour. Beware of any fish that is hollow bellied or looks as if it is wasting away; try and buy a fish that is swimming effortlessly and not one that is wobbling around uncertainly or skulking in the plants. Some fish may be suffering from travel sickness after their long journey to this country, so ask the dealer for his advice if you are at all unsure. It is not in his interest to sell you fish that might die — after all, he wants you to go back and buy from him next time.

You may find problems in identifying the fishes in your dealer's from the labels on the tank. The 'common names' of the pet shop may not tally with those in the library books which you may already have been reading. Remember that the commercial names may have been invented as a sales gimmick, whereas most library books will try to give the correct scientific name of the fish.

The hobby magazines are excellent sources of information and, being published monthly, are reasonably up-to-date and do give both common and scientific names. Dick was concerned about this problem for newcomers to the hobby and so together with aquarists from another Society he produced a Dictionary which cross-references all the common names against the scientific ones. There is nothing more frustrating than buying a new fish and then being unable to find out about it from the books because you don't know its proper name!

Feeding the Fish

Once you have chosen and bought your fish you will probably be given a plastic bag in which to take them home. The water in this bag may well differ in temperature from that in the tank, so to avoid shocking the fish by the change you must float the bag in the tank for a while to equalise temperatures. On no account should you tip the fish straight into the tank.

If you already have fish in the tank you will have to make some allowance for the fact that they will feel themselves to 'own' parts of the surroundings and will resent the intrusion of newcomers. When you bring your new fish home and after you have equalised the temperatures in his

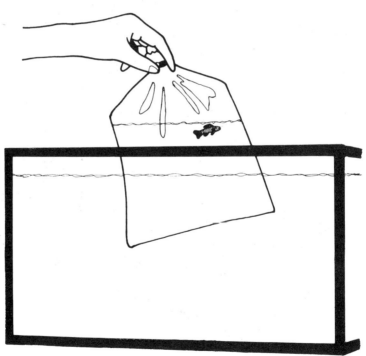

Equalising water temperatures before releasing new fish into the aquarium

bag and in the aquarium you can try one of two ways of introducing them to the tank. Firstly you could use food to attract the old fish to one end of the tank and insert new the new fish in the opposite end; alternatively you could try introducing newcomers at night when the lights are off and the fish are resting.

Feeding your fish is simple, and yet this is when most damage can be done, particularly if you overfeed — in fact it is easier to kill your fish by kindness than by neglect. The first rule is that you should establish regular feeding times and then feed only at these times; your fish will become accustomed to this and there is less danger of over-feeding. Dick usually feeds his in the morning before he goes to work, then again after he comes home at night, and finally he gives them a little bit before he goes to bed. I asked Dick about this feeding at night; wasn't that wasting food

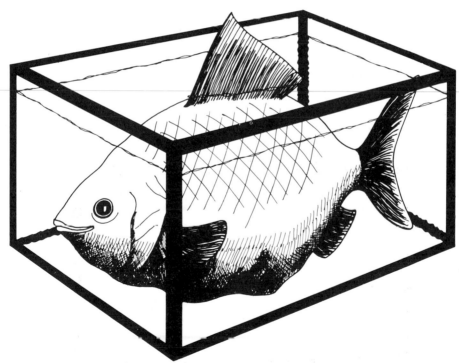

Overfeeding won't necessarily result in fishes like this — any uneaten food will pollute the tank before the fish can grow large

and perhaps risking polluting the tank with uneaten food? Not at all, he said, some fishes are naturally more active at night, so some food given at *our* bedtime may be regarded as *their* breakfast. Many of the catfishes and loaches are nocturnal creatures, and aquarists who specialise in keeping these particular fishes sometimes resort to strange devices in order to watch their fishes without having to stay up all night. What they do is to leave the tank lights burning brightly all night, then turn them down during the evening and hey presto, out come the fishes from their caves and hideaways thinking that it is night-time, little knowing that their owners are watching them from their favourite armchair. I have heard of that trick being played before, only this time at the London Zoo in the Nocturnal Mammal's House. Anyway, back to the feeding routine, how much do you give them to eat? Are fishes ravenous eaters, or do they just nibble around all day? Dick told me that while fish will not overeat, there is no point in putting in a large amount of food (to last while you are at school or work for instance) in the hope that the fish will leave a little for 'later on' — all that will happen is that the uneaten food will begin to contaminate the tank. At no time does he feed them more than they can eat in about two minutes. The second rule to follow is that only one member of the family should do the feeding. The great danger of all the family doing the feeding is that each person thinks the fish are hungry when they come up to the front of the tank and feeds them, not realising that the fish have already been fed.

Overfeeding can also be a problem at holiday time. If you ask the neighbours to look after the fish for you, make it quite clear how much food they should receive — you can even make up separately prepared meals for each day. You would be surprised how often people come home and find that out of kindness neighbours have fed two months' supply of food in a fortnight. In fact fish can survive quite easily for up to a fortnight without being fed and without artificial light, although with tropical fish you must remember to leave the heating on. Without lights the algae does not grow further, and if the fish become hungry they will eat the algae that is already there. So you might well return to find a clean tank and some very active and healthy fish.

How long can you expect your fish to live? That depends to a large extent on how well you look after them, but it should also be remembered that in their wild state some fish lay literally millions of eggs. This means that the life span of each individual fish can be fairly short but that the species will continue to thrive. Three to four years seems to be a reasonable life span for aquarium fish, although there are some that live many years longer; these are usually the breeds that lay fewer eggs and whose adults take the greatest care of their offspring.

How Fish Breed

The way fish breed is fascinating; full of variations and curiosities. Did you know, for instance, that some fish-mothers protect their young by packing them into their mouths like sardines in a can? Other fish protect their eggs by jumping out of the water to lay them. But before I go on to describe these oddities in more detail perhaps I had better first explain the two basic types of behaviour.

Dick told me that so far as breeding went the tropical fish world is divided into two groups — the livebearers and the egg-layers. Many of the easiest and most popular species — Guppies, Platies, Swordtails and Mollies — are livebearing fishes; that is to say, eggs develop within the females' bodies so that the mothers give birth to baby fish, in much the same way as mammals give birth to their young. As soon as they are born the young 'fry' head straight into the plants to protect themselves both from other larger fish and from their mothers, who tend to be cannibalistic. The livebearers can have a brood about once a month; in fact a female can have several successive broods from just one mating without being remated to a male. However, the young fish are easy prey for the adults, so you need have few fears about over-populating your tank.

If you wish to keep your young fish you should select the best and transfer them to another tank. By keeping only the fishes with the most desirable qualities (colour, fins, etc.) and ensuring that different colours do not interbreed with each other you should be able to develop attractive strains. Livebearing fish come in varied colours within the same species, but if these different colours mate with each other you may well end up with undistinguished mottled grey fish.

I have dealt with livebearing fish first, but in fact the more 'normal' way for fish to reproduce is for them to lay eggs. Some egg-layers scatter their eggs freely around the tank, and I am sorry to say that many of these eggs will end up as food for other fish. Others are a little more thoughtful, and this thoughtfulness leads to some of the oddities I mentioned earlier.

The Siamese Fighting Fish, a representative of the *anabantid* family of India and the Far East is among the more caring species. On the surface of the water the male builds a 'bubble' nest composed, literally, of bubbles

A male Siamese Fighting Fish *(B. splendens)* tending his nest

blown from its mouth and mixed with saliva. The eggs are laid below the nests and, being buoyant, float up and stick to it, to be guarded by the male until they hatch. Of course the Fighting Fish is noted for its ferocity, and this is one of the breeds where you must be careful not to let two males come together — otherwise they will literally tear each other to pieces in no time at all. Another speciality of these fish is that they have an auxiliary organ in their head which allows then to breathe air directly from the atmosphere, and for this reason it is quite possible to keep one fish in a small jam jar for display purposes whereas other species would suffocate because of the small surface water area. Have you seen jars of Siamese Fighting Fishes (one to a jar) in your pet shop? It's a handy way to keep the fishes separate from each other, yet in fairly large numbers for selling purposes; another advantage of this idea is that being next door to each other visibly, the Siamese Fighter male fishes are constantly 'showing off' belligerently to each other, extending their beautiful fins — not a bad advertising gimmick either, they're practically begging you to notice them and buy one. A word of warning from Dick: although you may see fish on display in small jars or tanks either at your shop or at fish shows, don't be tempted to think that they may be kept in such confined spaces comfortably for long. It is a bit like expecting people to live

27

comfortably in the equivalent of a tailor's shop window! Every fish needs, and deserves, the best that you can provide for it; only then will it feel comfortable and secure enough to behave naturally, thus giving you the pleasure that *you* want.

The popular Angelfish — a cichlid — and related to the perch found in Britain's rivers and canals — is another egg-laying species with special habits. A mother Angelfish will clean a stone, lay her eggs on it and then, helped by the male, with her fins fan the fertilised eggs until they hatch. After the fry are born they receive considerable parental care, the parents temporarily taking the babies into their mouths to clean them, and then herding the brood around rather like two sheepdogs guarding a flock. In fact some of these youngsters are guarded so well that all the other fish

A young 'half-black' Angelfish, a 'man-made' variety of this popular fish

are driven to the far end of the aquarium Angelfish are Dick's favourites and although he now has a great number of them, at one time he found it hard to breed them successfully. Following a number of failures — one of which nearly led to postponing a holiday — he joined his local aquarist club, and with the knowledge he gained there he was able to persevere with more success.

The so-called Mouth-Brooding Fish are also members of the angelfish's cichlid family. The peculiarity of these fish is that a female takes her eggs into her mouth to hatch them, keeping them there for anything up to two weeks. Showing great restraint the mother neither eats food nor devours her own eggs or young, and consequently she grows thinner and thinner. The young fish continue to receive this same protection after they have first left the mother's mouth: should there be the slightest hint of danger they are received back and crammed in.

Young Mouthbrooder fry emerging from the safety of their mother's mouth *(Haplochromis sp.)*

Perhaps the height of protectiveness is reached by the Splashing Tetra fish which leap out of the water and lay their eggs on an overhanging leaf where no other fish predators will be able to eat them. However, the parents are still burdened with the problem of keeping the eggs damp until they hatch; to achieve this the fish swim around beneath the leaves and splash water upwards.

In their natural habitats fish have to live under many peculiar conditions, and Dick told me about the marvellous adaptations made by the

'Annual Fish', which live in parts of the tropics where the rivers and streams dry up each year. The fish have evolved a system which ensures that although their eggs are laid just before the waters completely dry up they do not hatch until the beginning of the next rains (when the dry ditches become streams again). To ensure this the eggs are laid at the bottom of the river and remain in the mud when the drought comes, to be triggered into activity again when the rainy season starts. But this is not the end of it; the first rains often last only a day or two and are not enough to fill the river beds sufficiently for the fish to survive. The extraordinary mechanism within the eggs is accordingly developed so that the eggs have to be soaked twice — the second rains usually being the proper river-filling ones — before they will hatch.

In your aquarium you can create something similar to this life cycle. If you provide a peat covering to the floor of the tank or hang a nylon mop in it the annual fish's eggs can be kept in a semi-dry condition when they have been laid. After two or three months give them a soaking, and if they do not hatch out first time dry them off and then wet them for a second time just as would happen in the wilds. A clever way of making use of this ability of the eggs to survive periods of semi-dehydration is practised by enthusiastic aquarists the world over. Instead of just corresponding by letter to aquarist friends in other countries they also exchange fish-eggs! Just imagine how many letters you *don't* have to write describing your fishes to your friends — just send them the fishes themselves in egg form, and let them *see* what you're keeping in your tanks.

So fish-breeding is certainly one of the chief excitements of this hobby; more than that — because some of these fish breed so frequently and numerously you might well think it would be possible to make a bit of extra money by selling them to your petshop. However, the easier a fish is to breed the more people are going to do it and the less likely you are to be able to get rid of them. All right, you might think, let's try the unusual and exotic fish. Well there are some drawbacks here: firstly, you are going to have to acquire a great deal of knowledge, and you are going to have to give a great deal of care and attention to these specialised fish. Remember we are trying to use our ordinary tap water in which to keep fishes from different rivers, lakes and streams all over the world! And then even if you do succeed you might still find that your local dealer is not all that interested in your exotics, the reason being that he in turn will have fewer customers for unusual fish that are hard to keep. In general, then, it is not a good idea to enter this hobby planning to make money from it.

Piranhas and Other Fish

From page 72 onwards Dick recommends some of the fish you might like to buy when you first start fishkeeping; some of them are called by their scientific names, the names by which they are known internationally. These can be a little off-putting until you get used to them. Luckily most of our tropical aquarium fish also have easier English names like the guppies, mollies and angelfish I have already mentioned. Some of these names describe what the fish look like; for instance, there is the Tiger Barb which has four stripes which do indeed make it look like a tiger.

Before I met Dick I did not know an awful lot about this hobby, but one fish I could always recognise was the molly. These are always thought of as being black, and most people still seem to prefer this colour; however, they do also come in gold, green and silver. Indeed, it seems that man just cannot resist the temptation to tamper around with nature and will always try and develop new strains and colours. If enough fish of a particular species are bred there will sometimes be a freak fish, breed two of these together and you are on the way to a new fish. It is even possible now to find albino fish. Some ornamental goldfish have been so highly bred that if you put them back in the wilds they would not stand a chance — with their highly decorative fins they would never be able to swim fast enough to escape their enemies.

One very large family of fish is known as the *Characins.* Mostly, they come from South America and there is such a wide range of fish in this group that you would not imagine they were in any way related. One member is the extremely colourful Neon Tetra that has an electric blue flash along the top with a red line underneath. When they were first imported in the 1930s, they were so striking and attractive that they were not allowed to be exhibited in fish shows because it was felt that all the other fish would be put to a disadvantage! They are well accepted now and are a colourful addition to one's aquarium.

Another fish which has always interested me — though for rather a different reason — is the Piranha. There are great tales told of how shoals of these fish will demolish an animal or a human in seconds if they are unlucky enough to be swimming in the Amazon. When you see the speed

The Oranda, a fancy goldfish variety

This Piranha is unusual — it's got its mouth shut!

with which they eat a piece of meat or a small goldfish you might well believe these stories. However, they really look fierce and people do keep them, although as they grow to about eight inches long they need a fair amount of space. If you put a finger in the tank the piranha might come up to it but no more so than most fish that come and have a nibble. Like the shark, they tend to scent blood, so it might not be wise to offer a finger that is cut!

Talking of sharks reminds me of one other aquarium favourite — the Red Tail Black Shark whose home is the Far East. In fact, although this has a fin that looks similar to a shark it is not one at all — unlike its namesake it is mainly vegetarian. On the other hand it can certainly become aggressive in defence of its territory, choosing one piece of rock and keeping all other fish well away.

Caring for your Fish

As I have already said once you get your tank's balance right you should be able to keep you fish healthy. Some people believe that disease is always present in a tank and only breaks out when a fish for some reason weakens, if so the state of your tank will have a lot to do with whether or not this happens. Some pointers to remember are:
- do not overcrowd the aquarium
- do not over-feed
- avoid sudden changes in the temperature of the water
- keep together species that get along well
- keep the tank clean by siphoning out rubbish

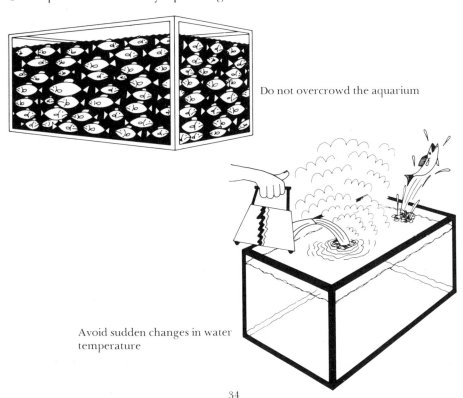

Do not overcrowd the aquarium

Avoid sudden changes in water temperature

Keep together species that get along well

If you follow these simple basic rules there is really not much to worry about and disease should not happen all that often. If it does, sometimes for the price of a cure you can buy a new fish, so you might well feel that if the fish is ailing badly it is better to replace it; it may indeed be kinder to kill it. Sometimes people do this by putting them down the lavatory, but this may well not kill the fish. Surprisingly, the quickest and kindest thing to do is to throw the fish as hard as you can on the floor. One important thing to remember if your fish does catch a disease is that none of these are transmissible to human beings.

One simple precaution to take with a fish that appears to be ill is to remove it from the main tank and keep it on its own while you treat it in a small 'hospital' tank. Indeed, if you have a second tank available it is a good idea to 'quarantine' any new fish in it for a week or two to make sure that they are all right before they are added to the aquarium. Although fish arrive from dealers on the other side of the world quite speedily, the journey can be a sudden shock to them. There could well be delayed flights and sometimes, for convenience, too many fish are put into one bag and they may even have been drugged first for the journey. As you can guess all this can be very upsetting for the fish. On the whole they are pretty hardy and do survive well but it is still wise to keep them apart from your main collection for a while if you can.

If your fish does get sick you should notice the symptoms and either look these up in a book or consult your dealer — there are many medicines available to cure your fish. Three of the commonest ailments are 'White Spot', 'Shimmying' and 'Fin Rot'.

Isolate sick fishes and quarantine all new additions

White Spot can sometimes break out if you move your fish too rapidly from one place to another. The symptoms are small white spots all over the fish's body — rather like our measles. Fortunately there is a good treatment available, and so if you follow the instructions on the bottle of medicine the fish will recover in a day or two.

A fish affected by the disease descriptively called 'Shimmying' will appear to be doing just that; swimming on the spot without getting anywhere. The cause may well be a drop in temperature, so in this case you should first check your tank's water temperature and adjust it where necessary.

Fin Rot sounds unpleasant, but is actually something that one fish inflicts on another when it bullies it by nipping and tearing its fins. The bacterial infection that sets in is the fin rot, rather like a cut finger that turns septic. Again, medicines are available, and in this case it is particularly advisable to remove the affected fish from the tank. If you do not have a spare tank, fill a plastic sandwich box full of water, put your fish in this and float this on the top of your aquarium. The water in the sandwich box will soon take on the temperature of the water in the tank. (A lot of aquarists think an excellent way to cure fin rot is to put a teaspoonful of natural salt to a gallon of water and let the fish swim in this. Do not use ordinary table salt, this has special additives to make it run out of your salt pot easily, and these can affect the water adversely.)

Clubs and Shows

Most people are quite happy just to have their aquarium somewhere in the house and derive enjoyment from watching and attending to their fish. A development of this is to do what Dick has done and use a garden shed so that you can increase the number of tanks. You may also remember that when I talked about the problems of breeding angelfish I mentioned that Dick got a lot of useful information as a result of joining his local aquarist's club. Well, there are about six hundred clubs throughout the country with annual subscriptions ranging from about £3.00 to £5.00, and I think it is well worth joining one. You find out how other members cope with problems similar to yours; there are guest lecturers as well as films, slide shows, visits and even trips abroad. Besides opportunities for learning more about the hobby, joining a club may also give you the chance of swopping fish and obtaining second-hand equipment (make sure it is in good condition). There is usually also a magazine which provides plenty of correspondence, not only with people in this country, but with aquarists throughout the world.

Another way to extend your hobby is to participate in fish shows of which there are at least two a week going on somewhere in the country from March until November. The size of these ranges from small ones in local village halls to competitions in large halls like the shows at Belle Vue, Manchester, Motherwell, Doncaster and at Alexandra Palace in London. There are no frills in these competitions — just the fish themselves each in its own glass tank, and there is no better way of seeing how yours compare with the best. I wondered how any one fish may be judged better than another, and who has to make the decision. To my uncritical eye, they all look good and, if you're like me with a soft spot for any animal, you'll know that I'd give every entry a prize! Dick explained that before any fish can be judged a system has to be worked out by which its merits can be evaluated.

Taking 100 points as a possible maximum, this total is divided into five groups of 20 points which are in turn maximum points for the following 'standards':

'Size' 20 points maximum if a fish reaches full size indicated for its species.

SHOW.	ANYTOWN OPEN SHOW		FEATURES POINTED.						JUDGES OVERALL QUALITY ASSESSMENT.	
DATE.	JULY '79								GOOD.	
CLASS No:	CHARACINS		SIZE	BODY	COLOUR	FINS	CONDITION & DEPORTMENT		AVERAGE.	✓
SHEET No:	2									
ENTRIES No:	18								POOR.	
EXHIBIT NAME.		TANK No:	20	20	20	20	20	TOTAL.	REMARKS.	
HYPHESSOBRYCON PULCHRIPINNIS LEMON TETRA		11	15	15	12	15	15	72	WOULD SHOW BETTER IN A DARK BOTTOMED TANK. POOR COLOUR	
HYPHESSOBRYCON SERPAE SERPAE TETRA		12	14	15	17	16	16	78	EXCELLENT COLOUR STILL HAS SOME GROWING TO COME	
HEMIGRAMMUS NANUS (HASEMANIA MARGINATA) SILVER TIPPED TETRA		13	15	12	18	15	16	76	DEFORMED BODY LET THIS ENTRY DOWN.	
PARACHEIRODON INNESI NEON TETRA		14	13	16	16	12	16	73	SMALL DORSAL AND ANAL FINS DAMAGED.	
HYPHESSOBRYCON ERYTHROSTIGMA BLEEDING HEART TETRA		15	17	14	15	16	13	75	SCALES DAMAGED BODY THIN GOOD SIZE.	
HYPHESSOBRYCON PULCHRIPINNIS LEMON TETRA		16	15	14	14	15	14	72	A YOUNG FISH WILL SHOW BETTER.	
PARACHEIRODON INNESI NEON TETRA		18	16	15	16	15	15	77	NICE FISH.	

A typical completed judging sheet from an Open Show *(Reproduced by courtesy of the Federation of British Aquatic Societies)*

The hall begins to fill up with exhibitors benching their entries; large letters denote various competitive classes

'*Body*' 20 again for a perfect body shape pertaining to the particular species. (Correct profile, no lumps or bumps; a tall body for angels for instance rather than a long one, and so on.)

'*Fins*' Must be all there! Some fishes may be born with fins missing. Fins must not be split, frayed or deformed.

'*Colour*' Must be natural (oh yes, hormone feeding is possible to accentuate colours) and must be dense. Any colour patterning must be precise, not running into other body areas with smudgy overlaps. In the livebearing fishes where selective breeding has produced many man-made patterns far removed from the natural wild fish's, these artifical standards must be observed.

'*Condition and Deportment*' For a moment I had visions of fishes swimming around with tiny books on their heads! Anyway, it is just what it says — a fish must be in good condition (a sick, diseased fish will be disqualified) and it must deport nicely, that is, it must not sulk in the corner of the tank or sit on the bottom with its fins folded up. You see, if a fish is not deporting properly, or showing itself well, a judge may not be able to assess many of its other characteristics either, so this deportment business is quite vital.

I was most surprised when, after I had lightheartedly suggested that perhaps aquarists ought to train their fishes for shows, Dick said that is exactly what some people do! I didn't know whether to believe him or not at first, but he was quite serious about it. He went on to explain that a fish must be unafraid of the people looking at it from the other side of the glass, and so it is quite the normal practice for a fish to be put into a bare show-type tank for a few hours at a time prior to a show, to get it used to the feeling of being in a smaller, unfurnished tank. If there are members of the household constantly passing the tank, the fish will soon get accustomed to people near it, and soon it will even come up to the glass to look at them!

Now that I have re-read all that, it begins to make sense, because once you know what the judges are looking out for then you are halfway to owning a champion! One other thing, the fishes are not all put together in one overall class; it is usual practice to divide the fishes at a Show into their natural family Classes, i.e. barbs, characins, cichlids, mollies, guppies, platies, swordtails, etc., and out of all the Class winners a 'Best Fish in Show' is chosen by the panel of judges. *Judges?* Well, yes; a Show can have upwards of 500 fish to judge in an afternoon so it makes sense to have enough judges so that the exhibitors are not kept waiting too long to find

Some of the glittering prizes to be won

out what they have won. Following a period of viewing the fishes at the end of judging, prizegiving soon takes place and then the exhibitors collect their fishes for the journey home. Already some of them will be planning the next Show where, this time, they're jolly well going to win!

Apart from the competitive side of shows, there are always lots of friends to be made, and Dick says many societies mutually support each other's shows up and down the country throughout the year. The result of these travels often means new fishes being introduced into new areas and this helps continue the freshness of the hobby. Fortunately, the prizes that are won are not enormous and so the competition is not quite so cut-throat as it appears to be in other 'animal' shows; there are no pedigrees involved and anyone can exhibit quite happily knowing that they do stand some chance of winning — providing they have done all the necessary preparation work!

The fish we have been talking about mainly, have been tropical fresh-water fish. Keeping saltwater tropical fish is not nearly so easy, which is a shame because like the freshwater fish they are fascinating and beautifully coloured. I know because I have had the marvellous opportunity on some of my travels in tropical parts of the world to go snorkelling. Once I mastered the breathing I found this one of the most enthralling things I have ever done and I have spent hours watching the brilliantly coloured world below me, swimming after the fish as they circled the coral and rocks. Those of you who live near the coast may have tried keeping the shrimps, anemones, crabs and other sea creatures from around our coast-line; for those away from the coast it is possible to buy the sort of salt that you add to ordinary water to create the consistency and chemical make-up of sea water. But once again you will need a thermostat and heater if you are going to try to keep tropical marine fish; really it is much better, as I have said, to start with a freshwater aquarium.

Well, I hope I have given you some sort of guide to the pleasure that awaits you in this hobby. Of course some people get very carried away with their aquariums and put all kinds of extra bits and pieces in — plastic flowers, underwater wrecks and windmills — turning them into dramatic aquascapes. I personally prefer to see aquariums looking attractive and simple — after all it is the fish that are most important and they should be the first things to catch your eye. A few rocks, plants and pieces of wood make much the best setting and you can have great fun arranging and rearranging them. Dick is still battling with the problem of keeping natural wood in his tanks without it going mouldy. Some people have no trouble but for some reason this is something Dick finds difficult, and that's the fascination of keeping fish — there is always something new to find out about and discover. Just when you might feel your interest is flagging along comes a fresh challenge: a new fish can trigger off a fresh set of problems which must be solved; a pair of fish suddenly present you with a few hundred baby fish and you have to find a spare tank for them. Fish you had maybe thought were dull or uninteresting unexpectedly reveal characteristics which completely change your mind and you are off again on a new adventure. Frequently you are updating ideas and techniques or trying new ways of doing things, and there is plenty of scope for you to become an 'authority' on one particular aspect of the hobby.

Fishkeeping, then, is a hobby anyone can enjoy and it will certainly provide you with hours of fascination and pleasure. Now I shall hand you over to Dick for his expert advice on the practical side of things. Best of luck with your fishes!

Useful Words

This section is intended to be used as a guide to some of the terms met with in the aquatic hobby which may be unfamiliar to the newcomer. Not all of the words contained in this Glossary may have appeared in this book, but you will probably soon encounter them when you persevere with the hobby.

Activated Carbon Special form of charcoal used as a filter material to absorb dissolved substances from the aquarium water.

Adipose (fin) A small 'extra' fin on the back of the fish, situated between the dorsal fin and the tail. Fishes carrying this fin include the majority of characins and catfishes.

Adult Fully grown, sexually mature.

Aeration The introduction of an air supply into the aquarium, to operate an airstone or filter.

Aerator Source of compressed air, usually a small electric, vibrator-type pump.

Airstone A block through which air is passed emerging as a stream of small bubbles.

Air Tubing Neoprene tubing through which air from the air-pump is supplied to the aquarium appliance.

Albino Lack of natural pigment, giving the fish a pinkish-white appearance; not found often in nature, more likely a result of selective breeding programmes by the hobbyist.

Algae Tiny primitive plants, which may grow as a troublesome covering in the aquarium, or may be suspended in the water, giving it a green cloudy appearance. Often encouraged by excess light, or too few plants.

All-glass Type of tank formed by gluing five panels of glass together with silicone sealant; no decorative or supporting frames.

Anabantid Group of fishes equipped with the additional organ which allows them to breathe atmospheric air; examples are the Gouramies and the Siamese Fighter.

Anal (fin) Single fin underneath the body of the fish immediately in front of the caudal fin (tail).

Annual (Fishes) Group of fishes which lay eggs in the mud so that the young may survive the complete drying up of the water in which the parents die. Killifishes.

Artemia Artemia salina, the brine shrimp. The eggs may be stored dry for long periods and then hatched in salt water by the hobbyist; the newly-hatched young shrimp form an ideal first food for the majority of young fishes.

Aquarist Person who keeps fishes, aquatic plants and other aquatic animals in captivity.

Aquarium Container in which fishes are kept; may refer to the completely furnished and stocked tank.

Aquascaping The action of furnishing a tank with gravel and rocks in an artistic way; in some cases may refer to furnishing the tank above the waterline with plants and ferns.

Barb Family of small bream-like fishes from India and the Far East. Usually identified by the small barbels around the mouth, although not all barbs have them.

Barbel Whisker-like growth around the mouth. In some fishes these whiskers have taste-buds by which the fishes taste the food lying on the tank floor.

Biological (filter) Type of filter which utilises bacterial action to break down toxic waste products into harmless nutrients. The undergravel filter (q.v.) works on this principle.

Bottom Fishes Any fish which naturally inhabits the bottom level of the tank; may be identified by their mouths which are underneath the head rather than at the body's extremity. Catfishes and loaches are good examples.

Brackish (water) Water that may become salty in nature, i.e. dykes and estuarine waters. In the aquarium, water that has salt added to it, but not as to make it as 'salty' as true sea-water.

Breeding-trap A small plastic tank with interior dividing panels in which a pregnant female livebearer may be placed to give birth, so that her young may escape from her and not be eaten. Usually suspended in the main aquarium. May cause premature births, by frightening the female, especially if used towards the very end of the pregnancy period.

Brine Shrimp (See Artemia).

Brood Collective noun often used to describe a hatching of livebearing fishes' young, or to the young of fishes which are cared for by the parents.

Buccal (cavity) Type of internal pouch below the jaw of mouthbreeding fishes, in which the eggs are held until they hatch and to which the young fry return when danger threatens.

Bulbs (lighting) Ordinary light bulbs, often called tungsten lighting.

Bulbs (plants)   The corm-like rhizomes of the Aponogeton plant family. These may be purchased during the plant's dormant period and produce leaves when immersed in the aquarium.

Cable-tidy   Trade name, or descriptive title, given to a small connecting junction box for electrical terminations.

Carbon   A substance used in filters. (See Activated Carbon).

Carnivorous   Meat-eater.

Catfishes   Collective name given to bottom-dwelling fishes which have well-developed 'whiskers', giving them a feline appearance. Very useful scavengers, but should not be kept solely for this purpose.

Caudal (fin)   The tail fin.

Caudal Peduncle   The tapered rear end of the fish which joins on to the tail, or caudal fin.

Characins   Large family of fishes which include the colourful Tetras and the fearsome Piranha.

Cichlids   Large family of fishes, related to the freshwater Perch, which contains the stately Angelfish; a highly evolved family which all practise parental care, despite their apparent pugnacious appearance.

Coldwater (fishkeeping)   Aquarium that is unheated. Adjective applied to any aquarium fishes, native or pond fishes, not needing a heated environment.

Compost   Alternative name for base covering of tank. (See Gravel).

Conditioning   The preparation of adult fishes for spawning, by the separation of the sexes and the feeding of prime foods. Also applied to water that has contained living fishes or plants and has therefore become 'conditioned'.

Corydoras   Genus of armoured catfishes from South America.

Cover-glass   A sheet of glass resting on top of the tank, but below the lamps. Prevents the hot lamps from becoming splashed, fishes from jumping out, and evaporation losses are minimised.

Cross-breed   (See Hybrid).

Crown   Part of plant where the roots meet the leaf stem; should not be buried.

Culling   The selection of young quality fishes from the whole brood and the discarding of the unwanted inferior ones.

Cuttings   Method of propagating plants by the severing of a leaf or stalk which then is self-rooting.

Cyclops   Small crustacean found in ponds and often caught for food by aquarists when seeking the more numerous daphnia (q.v.).

Danio   Small, shoaling fast-swimming fishes from India and the Far East. The Zebra Danio is an easy beginners' fish which is often recommended as your first spawning attempt.

Daphnia   The well-known 'water-flea', although it is not a flea at all. Sought-after live-food for aquarium fishes which may be caught in ponds and ditches during spring and summer.

Detritus   Uneaten food, fishes' waste products, dead leaves, etc., in short, all the rubbish at the bottom of the tank. Siphon it out!

Dimorphism (sexual)   Visual difference between the two sexes.

Dip-tube   A bell-ended tube used for removing detritus.

Dorsal   The fish's top surface, its back.

Dorsal (fin)   Single fin on top of the fish's back. Some species may have two, one behind the other but not to be confused with the adipose fin (q.v.) which cannot be moved voluntarily by the fish; dorsal fins can be moved.

Egglayers   Name given to those species of fishes whose eggs are laid and hatched outside of the female's body.

Exotic   Term generally given to non-native fishes, or to those fishes whose appearance has been exaggerated by selective breeding programmes.

Fancy Goldfish   Cultivated forms of the Common Goldfish.

Fertile   As applied to adult fishes, those which are sexually mature. As applied to fish eggs, those which have developing young inside.

Fertilisation   The act by which the eggs of the female are made active, by the contact with the male's milt. In livebearers this takes place inside the female fish; in egglaying species it occurs in the water of the tank.

Fighter   Normal abbreviation for the Siamese Fighting Fish.

Filaments   These are the extensions to the fins which normally the male species develop.

Filter   A device for mechanically, or biologically, cleaning the aquarium water.

Filter Wool   Any man-made fibre used for filtration purposes; glass-wool should not be used.

Filtration   Process by which the aquarium water is cleansed.

Fin Rot   Disease which appears literally to rot away the membrane of the fins; usually sets in after a fin has become damaged by accident, or by the attentions of a bullying fish.

46

Fins Equivalent to our limbs, may be 'paired' or arranged singly around the fish's body. They aid movement and stability. In livebearing species the anal fin (q.v.) is modified to form an organ with which the female fish is fertilised.

Fry The young of a fish.

Fungus A 'cotton-wool' like growth often found around the mouth of some fishes. A salt bath usually cures it.

Gallon Measure of liquid capacity. Weighs 10 pounds, and one cubic foot contains 6¼ gallons.

Gills Organ by which the fish breathes, extracts dissolved oxygen from the water. Situated on each side of the head.

Goldfish Carassius auratus.

Gonopodium The male livebearer's fertilising organ. (See Fins.)

Gouramies Group of fishes belonging to the Anabantid family; have the extra labyrinth organ in their head which allows them to breathe atmospheric air if required.

Gravel The material with which the base of the tank is covered; the medium in which the plants are rooted. Often called 'compost' or 'the substrate'.

Gravid Pregnant.

Hardness Measurement of dissolved solids in aquarium water. Example: rainwater is in most cases much softer (less hard) than water from the domestic supply.

Heater Small glass-covered electrical element which acts as an immersion heater.

Herbivorous Vegetarian.

Hood Tank cover which usually incorporates the light fittings.

Hybrid Young fish bred from parents of different species. Often infertile.

Ichthy (ology) Prefix (from the Greek, Ichthys — fish) therefore Ichthyology — Fish Study.

Inbreeding The repeated breeding of fishes from a common stock.

Infertile Unable to breed; or eggs which have not been successfully fertilised.

Infusoria Micro-organisms, cultured by the decay of vegetable matter in water, which form the first food for the tiniest of fry.

Killifish Group of fishes that occupy streams (killi — local word for ditch) which dry up annually; the eggs of these species can withstand drying out. (See Annual Fishes.)

Labyrinth (Fishes) (See Anabantid; Gouramies.)

Labyrinth Organ Additional organ with which some fishes are equipped which allows them to breathe atmospheric air. (See Anabantid; Gouramies.)

Lateral Line A row of pierced scales along the fish's flank through which vibrations are detected by way of links with the nervous system.

Laterally Compressed A thin fish — squashed from side to side, as in the Angel Fish.

Length Measured from tip of snout to end of caudal peduncle; tails are not included.

Litre Metric measure of liquid capacity equal to 1¾ pints Imperial Measure.

Livebearers Species of fishes where the eggs are fertilised inside the female's body, and develop there into fully formed fishes before birth occurs.

Loaches Elongated bottom-dwelling fishes, with erectile spines, from Asia.

Marbled Mottled patterning, usually of dark and white colours, covering the body, e.g. Marbled Angel, Marbled Hatchetfish.

Marine Pertaining to salt water.

Matt Opaque scale, in Fancy Goldfishes, giving a 'scaleless' effect.

Melanism A predominance of black, or dark, pigmentation.

Metallic Mirror-like scale, in Fancy Goldfish.

Milt The male fish's fertilising fluid.

Mops Bundles of nylon wool placed in the breeding tank in which eggs are caught; used mainly with Killifishes.

Mouth-breeder Species of fish where the female incubates the fertile eggs in her mouth. (See Buccal Cavity.)

Nacreous A sheen like 'mother-of-pearl' to fish scales; one of the three scale types in Fancy Goldfish. (See Matt, Metallic, Scales.)

Natural Selection The choosing of a mate by the fish themselves.

Nauplius Term mostly used to signify newly-hatched stage of the Brine Shrimp (q.v.)

Omnivorous Eats anything, meaty or vegetable matter.

Operculum   The external covering plate to the gills; also the plate which a snail uses to 'shut-the-shell' with when withdrawn into its shell.

Ova   Fish eggs.

Oviparous   Egglaying.

Ovipositor   Tubes (extended at breeding time) through which fishes such as Cichlids lay their eggs. Often used to describe the male's breeding tube through which milt is passed.

Ovoviviparous   Livebearing fishes; the fertilised eggs develop into miniature fishes within the female livebearer's body.

Peat-divers   Species of Killifishes (q.v.) which utilise a layer of peat on the base of their tank in which to lay their eggs.

Pectoral (fins)   Paired fins, emerging immediately behind the gills.

Pelvic (fins)   Paired fins, emerging on the underside of the fish ahead of the anal fin.

pH   Measurement of the acidity or alkalinity of aquarium water.

Photosynthesis   Process by which plants build up sugars and starches in their green cells under the influence of light, giving off oxygen and absorbing carbon dioxide in the process.

Power Filter   A filter system powered by small electric impeller rather than by air. Has higher water turnover (q.v.).

Propagation   Reproduction of young plants by various means. (See Cuttings, Runners.)

Quarantine   Advisable separation period of any new fishes or plants before adding them to the main aquarium collection; a safeguard against the spread of disease.

Rasboras   Large group of fast-swimming, colourful fishes from India and the Far East.

Rays   The many spines that support the fins.

Reticulated   A net-like patterning.

Rhizome   A tuberous root, or bulb (q.v.).

Rocks   Stone 'furnishings'.

Roe   Fish eggs.

Root   Underground anchoring and feeding system of plants.

Runners   Baby plants sent out along the surface of the gravel from the parent plant; may be severed and replanted to form new independent plants.

Salt   Sodium chloride. Use natural sea salt in aquatic uses.

Scales   Thin, bony overlapping plates covering the skin of fishes.

Scavengers   Fishes that are unfortunately kept solely for their 'clearing up' qualities, i.e. catfishes and other bottom dwellers.

Scraper   Device, utilising a razor-blade, used to remove algae growths from front glass of aquarium.

Scutes   Thicker armoured plates covering found in catfishes. (See Corydoras.)

Sealant   Modern silicone adhesive, capable of bonding panels of glass together; use in a ventilated area.

Sediment   Settlings of waste products, dead leaves, etc. (See Detritus.)

Seeds   Fruit of aquatic plants such as Aponogeton species.

Shimmying   Symptoms exhibited by fishes usually having been chilled; they appear to be weaving to and fro without any forward motion. Cure is simple, raise the temperature.

Shoal   Group of fishes of the same species.

Siphon   A device for transferring liquid automatically from one container to another which will continue as long as the source is higher than the destination. Siphons may be started by suction, as when emptying tanks into a bucket.

Spawning   Breeding.

Spawning Tank   Tank especially set up to receive a breeding pair, or team, of adult fishes, and in which the fry may be raised.

Species   Classification term used to denote allied groups of fishes.

Strip Lighting   Either: long tungsten bulbs, or fluorescent tubes.

Stripping   The removal of a female fish's eggs by hand; similarly a male fish can also be manually 'milked' of his fertilising fluid (milt).

Substrate   (See Gravel.)

Surface Area   Area of water surface in contact with the atmosphere.

Swim Bladder   'Buoyancy tank' within a fish which allows it to swim at all levels automatically without effort.

Tail   The caudal fin; the single fin at the rear end of a fish.

Tank   Watertight container with a transparent viewing panel.

Terminal (mouth)   Mouth situated at the extreme front end of a fish; not underslung, or upturned. Indicates a mid-water swimmer.

Territory   Area a fish decides to occupy to the exclusion of others.

Tetras   Group of fishes within the Characin family. (See Characins.)

Thermometer   Device for measuring heat.

Thermostat   Device for automatically controlling the heating device.

USEFUL WORDS

Tropical   Name applied to fishes (freshwater or marine) which require heated aquariums.

Tubercle   Small white pimples which male goldfish develop on their gill covers and head during the breeding season.

Tubifex   Small red worms found in river mud; may be bought in aquatic shops as live food for aquarium fishes. Should be kept under running water until fed to fishes.

Tungsten (lighting)   Conventional light bulbs.

Undergravel Filter   System of filtration which uses bacterial action in the aquarium gravel to break down waste products. Has to be installed first before gravel is added.

Variety   Differing colour patterns, or fin development, in fishes of the same species.

Ventral (fin)   (See Pelvic fin.)

Viviparous   (See Ovoviviparous.) Also applied to those livebearing species in which the developing fry obtain nourishment from the mother before birth.

Water-flea   (See Daphnia.)

Water-turnover   Rate at which water passes through a filter, i.e. rate at which the aquarium is cleaned (gallons per hour).

Wattages   Measurement of electrical power consumption; but taken as an indication of a lamp's brightness, for fishkeeping purposes. The higher the wattage, the brighter the lamp.

White Spot   A highly infectious aquarium disease which often occurs with the introduction of new stock. (See Quarantine.) Easily cured with proprietary medicines. Name describes the symptoms exactly.

Worms   First-class food for fishes. Size of worm offered depends on size of fish. Micro-worm, Grindal worm and White worm are all easily cultured by the hobbyist from commercially available starter 'kits'. Earthworms may be chopped or shredded for smaller fishes.

Understand the 'Whys' and 'Wherefores'!

Well, Val has given you some idea of the fascinations and attractions that fishkeeping offers. In this part of the book it is my job to give you some practical guidelines as to how to go about it.

You should remember that you cannot achieve maximum enjoyment from any hobby unless you understand the basic 'whys' and 'wherefores' right from the beginning. I have tried to present this section in as simple, 'non-fishkeeping' language as I can with the minimum of technical terms so as to introduce you to the hobby in as painless a way as possible. Please do not rush through this half in your haste to get cracking; it is all too easy to get off on the wrong foot, with the likely result that you will quickly become disappointed and consequently turn to another hobby, thus missing out on this truly rewarding one. I think I can truthfully say that no other hobby, particularly in the pet-keeping area, gives such a great satisfaction for such a *small* effort on the part of the hobbyist. Now that must be an encouraging state of affairs mustn't it? Let's look at this aspect first.

Fish are just about the most 'different' type of pet that you can hope to find. They live in a silent, mysterious world into which we cannot naturally intrude but only stand outside to observe and wonder at. However, this does have certain advantages; because we cannot share their world, *they* cannot share ours — hence they are never liberated from their 'prison'. It follows that we only need to tend to their living quarters and food requirements to keep them happy — it is almost a shame that the enjoyment seems to be a one-way experience.

It is important that we do keep the fish satisfied, because being held 'captive' they cannot escape from bad conditions or run away from home. They cannot even call for help! However, there are signs of distress which you will come to recognise, which you *must* take heed of, but these skills are acquired quite unconsciously and only involve your powers of observation.

Most of the so-called 'aquarium management' necessary — a rather intimidating expression — amounts to nothing more than applying a little commonsense, taking up only a few minutes of your time each day. The rest of the time spent on the hobby is genuine enjoyment! These few

What to strive for — a living picture

minutes a day, with perhaps a little longer at weekends, is a small price to pay for the rewards on offer, and they should not be regarded as a nuisance or a hindrance.

All of the hints and 'rules' given in the following pages have been tested over years and years of practical fishkeeping by the many thousands of aquarists who, by their efforts, have made fishkeeping a real possibility within the reach of everyone. The finest compliment we can pay these pioneers is to learn from them and be grateful.

The Tank and Gravel

Where to begin? Well, if you're going to keep fish you've got to keep them in something, so we might as well make a start with the tank itself. This may be the conventional box with all four sides and base made of glass, or it may be some other watertight container with only the one viewing panel made of glass. Whatever the size, shape or materials, one thing is now accepted by all aquarists — goldfish 'bowls' are strictly *out*.

The physical size of the tank is up to you (after all, you've not only got to afford it but also find room for it!), but an early rule is that a medium-sized tank is easier to maintain than a smaller, or larger, one. What's medium-sized? It's difficult to imagine 'so many gallons of water' as a shape at the outset, but a tank two or three feet long may be classed as 'medium', containing incidentally twelve gallons of water upwards. So now you know what size spaces to go looking for around the home!

Don't forget to allow room above the tank for the hood and cover (and room to raise it), plus some additional space around the sides of the tank to accommodate filters and air-pumps.

It is best to site a tank out of draughts and direct sunlight, so it follows that a vacant window-sill is not an ideal place. An alcove alongside a chimney breast is often chosen, but wherever it is put, a fully set-up tank is *heavy* (well over 1 cwt [51 kg]), so a firm, strong, level base is essential. *Never try to move a full aquarium*; if you don't strain yourself in the attempt it is likely that the changing pressures of water on the glass panels will result in a crack with dire effects!

Despite their inability to live outside their watery world, fish often seemingly make suicidal escape bids by jumping out of their tank, so a cover glass and a tank hood are needed, as Val explained on page 12.

The number of fish that can be kept in a tank does not depend upon its total capacity of water. Far more an influencing factor is the shape of the tank, or rather its water surface area. Two tanks of equal volume will hold two widely differing totals of fish; imagine two oblong tanks, one stood on end, the other lying flat with its longest side horizontal. The longer low tank has a far greater water surface area than the tall tank. Because the all-important oxygen enters the water from the atmosphere at the water's surface, it follows that the greater the water surface area the more oxygen

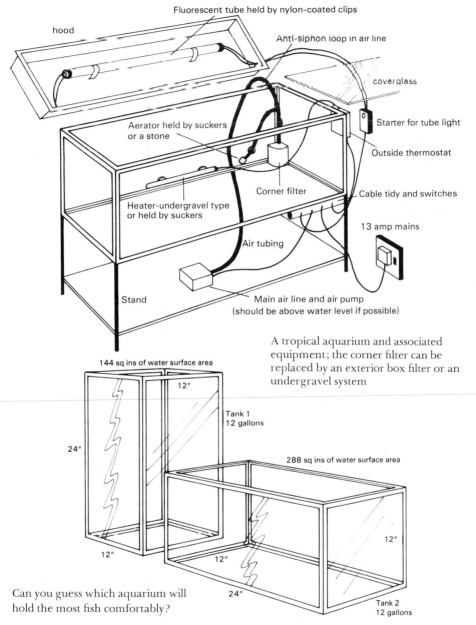

Fluorescent tube held by nylon-coated clips

hood

Anti-siphon loop in air line

coverglass

Aerator held by suckers
or a stone

Starter for tube light

Outside thermostat

Corner filter

Cable tidy and switches

Heater-undergravel type
or held by suckers

13 amp mains

Air tubing

Stand

Main air line and air pump
(should be above water level if possible)

A tropical aquarium and associated
equipment; the corner filter can be
replaced by an exterior box filter or an
undergravel system

144 sq ins of water surface area

12"

Tank 1
12 gallons

24"

288 sq ins of water surface area

12"

12"

Tank 2
12 gallons

12"

12"

24"

Can you guess which aquarium will
hold the most fish comfortably?

can enter. Tropical freshwater fish need about 8 sq. inches (50 sq. cm) for
every inch of body length; coldwater fishes need over three times this
amount (the fish's tail doesn't count in any measuring). Now you can see
why a goldfish shouldn't be kept in a bowl.

Another interchange of gas takes place at the water surface and is just as important (perhaps more so) than the passage of oxygen. Just like us, fish 'breathe' out carbon dioxide and this gas must be given every opportunity to escape or to be utilised and got rid of in other ways. As it escapes only slowly compared to the intake of oxygen, again a large surface area will help to disperse this unwanted gas. We will return to this subject later on, when you will see how the whole aquarium is dependent upon its many parts.

Turning aside for a minute from the theory, one worry for perhaps every new aquarist (or certainly a young aquarist's mother) is 'Will the tank leak?' or, 'What should I do if it does?' We all know how much mess a pint of milk makes when spilt, so a dozen gallons of water should be a veritable flood! Happily, leaks are the exception rather than the rule; those that occur in new tanks made of iron frames with putty and glass usually seal themselves as the glass and putty bed themselves in. Modern 'all-glass' tanks with silicone-sealed bonded panes of glass seldom leak but should this occur the leak may be re-sealed using a small amount of the sealer. As long as the filled tank is not disturbed and is set on a firm foundation the novice aquarist should sleep easily. I have had only one mishap in nearly twenty years of fishkeeping and that was my own fault — I accidentally hit the front glass of a tank when moving something near it, but a swiftly placed bucket caught most of the water! This should remind us that most of fishkeeping is based on commonsense rather than science!

Back to the fishes' requirements, and another thing to bear in mind is that we are trying to create an environment in which the fish will not only survive but, we hope, will feel 'at home' and secure enough to want to raise a family. Thus, while we prepare the tank we must think of the fishes' needs all along the line until we get to that great moment when we add them to the completed, set-up tank. We have already considered giving the fishes enough room in which to live and now we can move on to prepare the 'furnishings'.

Let us take a look at an aquatic scene from bottom to top, a logical order since it is in the sequence of events of furnishing a tank.

The bottom of the tank is usually covered with a layer of *gravel*, small stones about 2—3mm in diameter. Some books may call this material 'compost', others 'the substrate', but whatever you care to call it, it goes in first!

Gravel serves several purposes. Firstly it gives the fish a dark-coloured base to swim over, and this is naturally correct, for a fish's back is

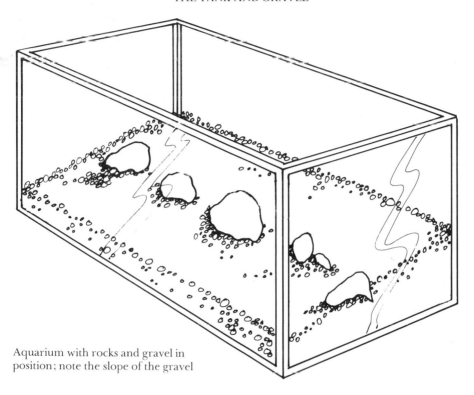

Aquarium with rocks and gravel in position; note the slope of the gravel

generally the darkest part of its body so that it merges against the dark bed of the river, helping to camouflage the fish against would-be predators. The fish does not lose its fears just because it is in a safe, 'indoor' home. If the base of the aquarium is not covered, the glass 'floor' would act as a mirror reflecting light back up under the swimming fishes, giving them a very pale, 'washed-out' appearance — hardly a colourful sight. Aquatic plants need some base material into which to root, and gravel serves this purpose nicely. Lastly, a form of filtration (see page 64) utilises the base material in its operation, so a covering of gravel is essential in this respect.

How much gravel? A rough guide is about a bucketful per square foot of tank floor area. A 'landscaped' base looks better than a flat layer, and the gravel should be sloped from the back down to the front of the tank; it may be 3 to 4 inches deep at the back and only 1 inch at the front. This natural slope also enables any dirt or uneaten food to collect where it is easily seen and from where it can be removed by means of a syphon tube.

Rocks can be used as 'fences' to hold banks of gravel in place but these rocks should be standing on the tank base to give them stability (some fishes are keen diggers and could easily topple a rock only perched on top of the gravel).

Gravel should be washed free of dust before putting it into the tank; a bucket half full of gravel is washed under a running hose until the water comes off clean. This process is best done outdoors; try not to tread gravel back indoors — it's fine for fish tanks but not too kind to carpets! When your 'aquascaping' is complete with rocks etc., don't ruin your handiwork by flattening the whole lot when you tip the water in; stand a small cup, saucer or basin on the gravel and introduce water into this so that it overflows gently into the tank without disturbing the gravel.

Plants

Right! Now that we have provided the 'carpet' in the fishes' living room, how about some furniture? There is no reason why fish should be kept captive in bare containers, and furnishings in the form of rocks, logs and plants are not only pleasing to see but also add to the fishes' comfort.

Rockwork can be used to build caves and crevices where those fish used to such surroundings in nature will feel at home. It affords fish some opportunity for privacy should the need arise to say nothing of a refuge from a larger, bullying neighbour. Remember Val's few words of warning concerning the selection of rocks for the aquarium (page 15). Slate, sandstone and quartz are all safe choices.

Similarly, a submerged log may look exactly natural but any wood used must be long dead and previously well waterlogged if possible. Several long immersions in boiling water will help kill off any doubtful wood and a few weeks soaking in several changes of fresh water (before introduction to the aquarium) will ideally prepare the chosen woodwork. It is possible to purchase petrified wood, cork-bark and even simulated life-like logs for tank decoration from your normal aquatic dealer.

Why not fabricate a rock-wall on to the rear wall of the tank by means of the silicone-sealant/adhesive, and if any rockwork doesn't quite conform to your requirements naturally, pieces may be glued together to achieve your planned design. One thing to avoid doing is to create 'fish-traps' where a fish can get caught and die unnoticed — its decaying body will soon pollute the tank.

Some people fancy sea-shells as tank decorations, but these can cause problems with the water becoming 'harder' due to the chemical composition of the shells, so they are best omitted from the freshwater tank.

With all this rockwork and sunken logs, we must not overcrowd the tank, we must leave some room for the fish to swim!

A living, growing natural tank decoration is provided by the aquatic plants which contrast nicely against the colours of the gravel and rocks. They not only complete the visual appeal of the aquarium but also help keep the water sweet — another way of saying to make the aquarium conditions more suitable for the fish. We now return briefly to the carbon dioxide disposal question.

Plants, under illumination, absorb the carbon dioxide breathed out by the fish — a highly satisfactory arrangement. As we have seen earlier, as carbon dioxide is not easily dispersed at the water's surface this facility of the plants to absorb it is very welcome and another good reason for having plants.

Other functions of plants are to give the fishes shelter, some assistance in breeding and, in some cases, food! A nearby bushy plant is a handy hideaway for timid fish, whilst the dense foliage also serves as a spawning medium in which the fishes' eggs can be caught. Vegetarian fish like to nibble the soft-leaved varieties of plants, so some thought has to be given to the choice of plants when such fish are intended to be kept. Imitation, plastic plants are perhaps the answer for the aquarist who wants 'greenery' in his tanks but also wants to keep vegetarian fish or those fish whose digging habits preclude the inclusion of natural plants in the tank. Purists may scorn such additions to the aquarium but when covered with a natural covering of algae these 'impostors' (the plants, not the purists!) do take on a more natural appearance — the only snag is that they do not fulfil the same carbon dioxide dispersing function as the real thing.

Aquatic plants come in every shape and size. Bushy clumps disguise the fact that the aquarium is nothing but a glass box by hiding the corners. Rock-work can poke out from amongst tall grass-like forests whilst overhead a raft of tiny leaves give shade from the perpetual 'sun' of the lamps. Larger, more robust varieties provide a base on which some fishes lay their eggs, and low, broad-leaved types give a lawn effect over the gravel — bottom-living fishes spend many happy hours under such plants, especially when you want to catch them!

It is quite possible for the aquarist to grow his own future stocks of plants from his original purchases. Plants reproduce in several ways: by cuttings, by sending out runners which develop into baby plants, or by seeds from flowers (for the more experienced aquarist). None of these methods occur if the original plant is not cultured properly.

Floating plants may need protecting from the heat of the tank lights by a cover glass, otherwise their leaves may be scorched: rooted plants should be grown with the junction between plant stem and root system just above the gravel surface, otherwise any part of the stem or leaf that is buried may rot away and the plant will die. Cuttings may be weighted down with a lead wire or simply pushed into the gravel where they will root and continue to grow. The plant from which cuttings are taken will be encouraged to grow more bushy as a result of regular 'pruning'. Some plants have a 'bulb' or corm-like structure instead of roots; this may be

The Amazon Sword Plant *(Echinodorus paniculatus)*

Spiral Vallis *(Vallisueria spiralis)*

Water Wistaria *(Hygrophila difformis)*

Cabomba   *Hygrophila polysperma*

buried in the gravel, and it is normal for these plants to have a natural resting period during our winter months irrespective of the conditions in the aquarium, so don't worry if these plants appear to die down regularly.

Now that we have finished furnishing the tank, it might be reasoned that due to the plants consuming the carbon dioxide, and the fishes' waste products feeding the plants, everything is in a nicely balanced state, and that all we have to do to keep it going this way is to add a pinch of food. Unfortunately it is a fallacy that an aquarium is a section from a natural aquatic scene; our indoor tank is not subject to the seasonal changes and climatic influences as is a river or a pool in the wild. To emulate Mother Nature we need to employ artificial aids in order to bring our aquarium conditions up to natural specifications.

Heating

If it is intended to keep tropical fishes, then the water must be kept warm and this involves some form of automatic heating system. Many people are put off at this stage, expecting that the technicalities will be too much for them but, if you stop to think for a minute, there aren't many people whose lives are not affected somewhere by a thermostatically controlled electrical device, be it a refrigerator, central heating system, electric iron, cooker, etc.

The heating system for an aquarium is just as simple, reliable and forgettable! The only provisos to bear in mind are:

1. Make all connections and adjustments with the power switched off.
2. Do not switch on a heater unless it is underwater.
3. Do not put your hand in the tank without first switching off the power — but remember to switch it back on again afterwards.

The size (wattage) of the heater should be suited to the size of the tank; a large heater will *quickly* overheat a small tank should the thermostat fail to switch off at the required temperature, whereas a small heater will be 'on' all the time trying to cope with a large tank. Two heaters can be used (one at each end of the large tank) and will operate quite satisfactorily from a single thermostat.

There are now available heater 'mats' on which the whole tank is stood operating on a safe, low voltage.

The thermostats are generally adjusted at the factory to operate around the 75°F (24°C) mark, the normal tropical fish aquarium temperature. There's no need, therefore, to worry about the complexity of technicalities.

Lighting, Air Pump and Filters

Arranging the lighting is equally simple, and lamp bulbs and fluorescent tubes may be used successfully, either separately, or in combinations of the two. We have already seen that light is necessary for the plants' growth and for us to be able to see our pets. The only thing to worry about seriously is getting the *amount* of light adjusted correctly.

Most indoor tanks are lit from breakfast to suppertime (for the benefit and convenience of the aquarist!) and the intensity (wattage) of the light should be chosen to give good plant growth without any undesirable growth of algae appearing. Some experimentation may be needed to achieve the right balance between the length of time of illumination and the light intensity, but don't be afraid to try different lighting arrangements. There are fluorescent tubes available which are said to be specially suitable for plant growth, but some hobbyists find that ordinary bulbs or 'warm-white' tubes are just as effective.

Often, if algae is growing too well for your liking a cut-back in light (either in period or intensity) will stop its remorseless progress throughout the tank; sometimes all that happens is that your plants die! In this case, try leaving the light alone and add some *more* plants to help crowd out the algae. Of course, we mustn't forget that algae can form an important part of the vegetarian fishes' diet, so a little may be left to grow on the side and rear walls of the tank for their benefit. Any algae on the front glass can be removed using a scraper.

Most newcomers to fishkeeping expect to see movement in the tank in addition to that provided by the fishes; this seems to manifest itself in a column of bubbles provided by an air-pump and an airstone. This is not obligatory, but it does introduce other influences into the tank which can add to the fishes' well-being.

The introduction of air into the aquarium does not oxygenate the water through the air bubbles any more than do 'oxygenating' plants. What does happen is the movement caused by the bubbles 'turns over' the water surface helping to disperse carbon dioxide and allowing fresh oxygen to enter. Aeration effectively enlarges the water surface area and although this allows more fishes to be kept than would be possible in a similar-sized unaerated tank, you should not stock your tank using this as a guide. If

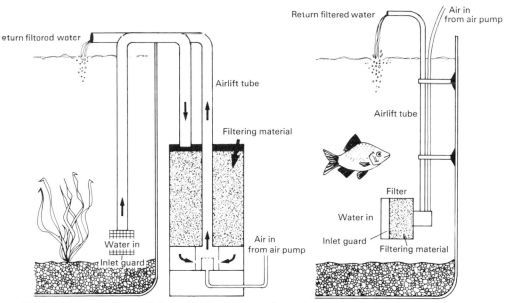

Two air-operated filters: *(left)* outside box type, *(right)* inside box type

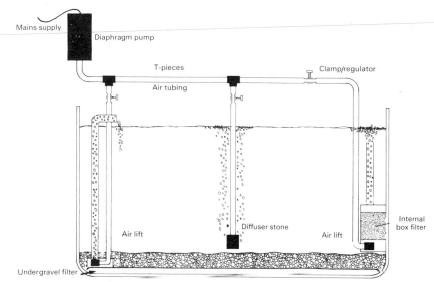

How various air-operated devices may be connected to work from a common air supply and yet be individually controlled

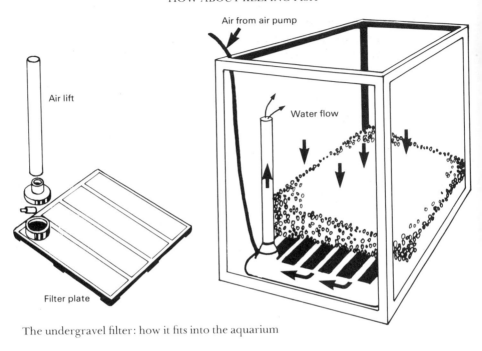

The undergravel filter: how it fits into the aquarium

your air supply fails then your tank suddenly becomes overcrowded and the fishes suffer.

As well as supplying those ever-moving bubbles, air can be used to operate other artificial aids, such as *filters*. Filtration involves cleaning the aquarium water by passing it through a box in which there are substances which remove unwanted dirt from it. Filter wool (generally man-made fibre material) traps dirt floating in suspension in the water, whilst a certain type of carbon (known as 'activated carbon') removes dissolved minerals.

The box containing the filtering medium may be either situated in the tank itself or outside, although for easy maintenance the outside type is more practical.

Filters are extremely logical pieces of equipment and simple to install, but this very simplicity often leads to complacency and neglect by the fishkeeper. Whilst a dirty filter indicates that it is doing its job, an over-dirty one is probably doing more harm than good, so do clean them regularly.

A form of filter which uses no boxes or filter-wool is the *undergravel* type. As its name implies, this device works beneath the gravel and if you intend to use this type of filter it has to be installed in the bare tank right at the beginning before you add the gravel. Air from the air-pump is used to draw water down through the gravel to the filter tubes or plate; colonies of suitable bacteria are encouraged to develop in the gravel by the oxygen-laden water flowing through it and these bacteria decompose otherwise toxic substances into less harmful forms. When using this type of filter **do not switch off its air supply** otherwise the colonies of bacteria will die off creating even more problems. As you progress in the hobby you will find that great arguments rage over the advantages or dis-advantages of undergravel filtration in freshwater aquariums. I find that it is best to decide on what works best for your set of circumstances — and stick to it! Having said that, don't be afraid to try new ideas; you may find that certain fish, or plants, need slightly different conditions and this 'experimentation' is the very heart of the hobby.

Summary

At this point, a brief summary may not come amiss:
1. The tank has been set up in its final position (not near a window, or on a flimsy table).
2. Washed gravel and rocks have been landscaped (undergravel filter fitted first? No sharp-edged rocks, no 'fish-traps').
3. Necessary 'hardware' installed (heater, thermostat, filter, lights, air-pump).
4. Water. The tank may be $\frac{3}{4}$ filled at this time — the empty $\frac{1}{4}$ is to allow for your hands and arms when planting. (You can try the heating system now, but **switch off whenever** your hands are to go into the tank.)
5. Add the plants (plant generously; you'll need two or three dozen grass-like plants at least for a 2 ft tank, in addition to the bushy types and featured specimens). After planting, add the rest of the water to completely fill the tank.
6. Switch it all on, lights as well, and then leave well alone for a week or two. Treat the aquarium just as if it had fish in it, switching the lights on and off each day. You won't need to add food, of course (this would soon pollute the uninhabited tank); this empty period enables the tank to settle down. The plants will root, without the fish disturbing them; the water will have lost its newness and become 'aged' and by the time you have read the rest of this book and learnt how to choose your fish (and what sort you want) the tank will be just right to receive them.

Food and Health

Just before we complete the picture by introducing the types of fish available to you, you should know how to look after them, and what characteristics to look out for when choosing fishes.

Enough hard work and research has been done over the years by fishkeepers and scientists to enable us to give our fish a suitable diet just by opening a tin or packet. Modern manufactured fish foods are completely reliable and nutritious, with a variety of diets available for different families of fishes. A mixed diet is highly recommended, not only between the various brands of dry foods but also by the addition of 'live' foods. 'Water Fleas', gnat larvae, earthworms (chopped if necessary!) special worm cultures, which can be multiplied by the aquarist, are all relished by the fishes. Brine Shrimp are particularly valuable for baby fishes; these shrimps can be hatched from their dried eggs quite simply by the aquarist, resulting in a tiny, live, disease-free food which is ideal. Household scraps can be offered to adult fishes — lean scraped meat (raw or cooked), lettuce, peas, cereal foods, cheese, fish meat and roe, etc. No fish need ever go hungry!

With all foods, do not be over-generous; follow the advice given by Val on page 24. 'A little and often' is far better than a large portion at once. Food cannot be set aside for 'later on' and any uneaten food is a danger to the tank's cleanliness. Give as much food as the fish will eat in a few minutes only. If you decide to share a tank with your brothers and sisters do make sure that they know when you've 'just fed the fish'.

Speaking of fish losses, is a reminder of fish illnesses. Not all are fatal by any means, and we can't catch them anyway! If we briefly mention a few symptoms a fish may show, you'll know what to look out for. A good time to check your fishes is when they come out for food, and it doesn't take long to see if they're all healthy and fighting fit.

Sometimes a fish may develop spots, ragged fins, cotton-wool like growths or just be constantly rubbing themselves against rocks or plants as if they had an itch. These are all symptoms of fish diseases or parasitic infection. Luckily, proprietary brands of remedies and cures are commercially available, easy to use and quite effective. We shall not dwell overlong on this subject; suffice to say that unfortunately such things

Two widely used 'live' foods for aquarium fishes

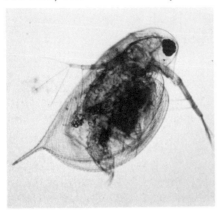

The Water 'Flea' *(Daphnia pulex)*

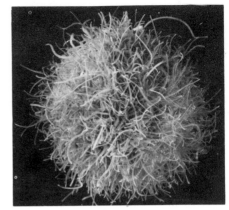

Tubifex Worms

occur even in the best maintained tanks and we should be prepared for them.

When we go to buy a fish what should we look for, to ensure that the fish is healthy?

Obviously a fish must be able to swim normally without any wobbly movements or sideways floating. Just as you would tend to choose a lively, alert puppy so do you look out for a fit and bright fish. No folded fins, no sulking or hiding in the corner of the tank; its colours should be definite, clearly defined and not patchy; certainly it should not have a 'hollowed' appearance. Try not to buy any new stock immediately it makes its appearance in the shop, unless you know for a fact it has been quarantined; the dealer should not mind you asking! With your first collection you will be virtually quarantining all your new fish in their new home, but after these have settled down you should quarantine any subsequent new purchases in a separate tank for a week or two before adding them to your aquarium. Strictly speaking, this procedure should be followed for plants too.

The dealer will give you the fish to take home in a plastic bag; if the journey is fairly long it might be better to carry the fish home within an insulated box to prevent heat loss, or slip the plastic bag inside your coat. At home, don't tip the fishes straight into the aquarium; the difference in the temperature between that of the water in the plastic bag and that of your tank may shock the fish. Instead, follow the procedure explained by Val on page 22.

What are Fish ?

Now for some facts about the fish as an animal, quite different from ourselves. We have already mentioned that their world is different from ours and that they breathe dissolved oxygen by means of *gills*. The paired *fins* of a fish correspond to our arms and legs and are used in manoeuvring, whilst the single fins assist in motion and stability.

The *mouth*, used for breathing as well as feeding, may be situated in either one of three positions depending on where the fish normally feeds. An upturned mouth is ideally suited for plucking insects from the water surface and usually belongs to a surface swimmer; a middle mouth, on a horizontal line from snout to tail suggests that its owner swims around the middle layers of the water, whilst an underslung mouth (often with bristly barbels and thick fleshy lips) indicates the fish is a bottom dweller, or feeds from the surface of rocks or algae-covered plants.

Similarly, *body shapes* also tell you about the fishes' swimming habits. Torpedo shape — fast swimmers; disk shape — more graceful, slower moving fishes often found in amongst tall aquatic plants; fishes with a flat bottom to their bodies are naturally suited for hunting for food at the bottom of the aquarium. To return to the sucker-mouth fishes for a moment, these are inhabitants of fast-flowing streams and use their mouths to hang on with to avoid being swept away: one of these fish breathes not through its mouth but through a special opening in the top of its head.

The size of a fish's *eye* may give you some idea how large it may grow (rather like the size of a puppy's paws which also act as a guide as to its final size) and also from what type of natural habitat it comes — big eye, generally dark murky water, plenty of plants maybe. Incidentally, fishes' eyes need no eyelids to protect the eyes from drying out, as ours do, since the fish is permanently wet!

Fish also have all sorts of extra 'accessories'. In the heads of some there are special chambers that allow them to breathe atmospheric air should their own environment become stagnant; in others electricity generating cells to help guard against predators, or perhaps to be used as a weapon. Others are equipped with magnetic field generators which give radar-like navigation assistance in murky waters where even the biggest eyes are of

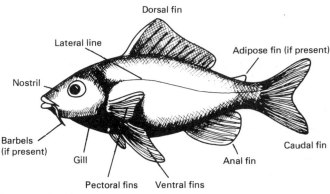

The external features of a fish

little use; and finally there is an automatic buoyancy tank known as the *swim bladder* which allows the fish to remain at any depth without having to make a swimming action all the time.

Fishes can hear, although they have no visible ears. They have a very delicate sensory system which has its detectors appearing like a row of portholes along each side of the body. This, the *lateral line* system, picks up the slightest vibration in the surrounding water, telling the fish that something is approaching, or that the airstone is nearby: another reason not to tap on the aquarium glass, or even slam the door of the room containing their tank.

From all this, you can see that fish are complicated animals, in addition to just being decorative. However, it is probably on a purely decorative basis that your original fishes will be chosen, so now is the moment you've all been waiting for: let's meet the fish!

Types of Tropical Aquarium Fish

Livebearers

Most non-fishkeepers will have heard of the *Guppy,* so we may as well make it the first on the list.

The Guppy *(Poecilia reticulata)*

Native to Venezuela, Trinidad. A member of the group of fishes known as *'Livebearers'.*

This group give birth to living, fully-formed youngsters after a development time of about a month inside their mother's body.

Guppies are sometimes known as 'Millions Fish' and they do seem to

A pair of Sailfin Mollies *(Mollienesia velifera),* male above

Pair of Swordtails *(Poecilia helleri)*, male on the left

come in as many colour varieties and patterns with no two males looking exactly alike.

A very hardy fish, a prolific breeder, it is found in other tropical parts of the world where it has been imported to eat mosquito larvae, thus controlling the spread of malaria.

The Molly *(Poecilia sphenops)*

Native to Southern USA and Mexico.

Another popular livebearer, generally available in the all-black form, although there are also green and gold varieties.

The Swordtail *(Xiphophorus helleri)*

Central America, Mexico and Guatemala.

Aptly named for the males do carry a swordlike appendage; not at the front like the marine swordfish but as an extension to their tail. Many colour varieties available.

The Platy *(Xiphophorus maculatus)*
  Mexico.
  A very close relative of the Swordtail and is a smaller, plumper swordless version.
  Again, many colour patterns are available.
With these prolific livebearing species you can almost plan what colour fish you will get from breeding, or what finnage the fish will have. Recognised colour patterns have become established through selective breeding programmes, and there are specialist Societies for aquarists only interested in these livebearing fish.

Most livebearers appreciate some vegetable matter in their diet but this is easily provided by adding to their normal food intake chopped spinach, lettuce, peas, wheat-germ or even scrapings of algae.

The four species of fishes just outlined make up the majority of livebearing fishes kept in aquariums, but there are many other not so well-known species of livebearing fishes that are often available, increasingly so due to the efforts of dedicated aquarists who are keeping and breeding these rarer fishes.

Egg-layers

All the other fishes kept in aquariums are 'egg-layers', where the eggs hatch outside the female's body, more often than not unattended. Within this group there are several different methods of reproduction, even a fish that lays its eggs out of the water!

A popular family of fishes are the **Barbs**, so named after the tiny barbels

The attractive *Barbus lineatus,* Striped Barb

Black Neon Tetras *(Hyphessobrycon herbertaxelrodi),* male above

around their mouth; these small Bream-like fishes are very colourful and active, some are so full of 'joie-de-vivre' that they tend to disturb the other inhabitants with their boisterousness, but they mean no harm. Popular Barbs (from India, Burma and the Far East) include the *Tiger Barb* (Barbus sumatranus), *Cherry Barb* (B.titteya), *Checker Barb* (B.oligolepis), *Ruby Barb* (B.nigrofasciatus) and the *'Schuberti' Barb* (B.semifasciolatus), the last named being a gold variety of a naturally green fish.

Equally numerous in choice and colourations are the South American **Characins**. This group includes the diminutive Tetras, the *Neon Tetra* (Cheirodon innesi), *Cardinal Tetra* (C.axelrodi), the *Lemon Tetra* (Hyphessobrycon pulchripinnis) at one end of the scale, through the striped colours and torpedo-shaped bodies of the *Pencilfishes* (Nannostomus and Poeciliobryon species) to the notorious *Piranhas*, quite surprisingly capable of being kept as an aquarium fish!

The Barb and Characin groups reproduce mostly by scattering their eggs into the water. Apart from the *Splashing Tetra* (Copeina arnoldi) which lays its eggs out of the water on an overhanging leaf (and then has to splash the eggs regularly to prevent them dehydrating!), and its immediate relatives which lay eggs on submerged plants and guard them, little parental care is exercised.

Much higher in evolutionary terms comes the **Cichlid** family. The *Angelfish* (Pterophyllum scalare) from the River Amazon, a familiar fish

A pair of Oscars *(Astronotus ocellaris)*. The young Oscar is a pretty, marbled fish, but it grows very large (and uglier) with age

with its tall fins and graceful movements, along with its near neighbour the stately *Discus* (Symphysodon discus) share the family group with the more representatively stocky and, to all appearances, more robust natured characters such as the *Blue Acara* (Aequidens pulcher) and the *Oscar* (Astronotus ocellaris). The smaller, brightly coloured Dwarf Cichlids from South America compete for your attention with their brilliantly hued cousins from Africa's Great Rift Valley Lakes. The Cichlids exercise great parental care in looking after their carefully laid eggs and subsequent offspring, as Val describes on page 28.

The **Anabantid** fishes from the Far East include the famous *Siamese Fighting Fish* (Betta splendens) well-known for its pugnacity to other male Siamese Fighting Fish and also for the beauty of its fins: reds, blues and green colours are often found, all results of the aquarist's skill in breeding programmes with these fishes. The quiet and peaceful **Gouramies** add dignity and grace to the aquarium and notable examples are the *Honey Gourami* (Colisa chuna), the *Dwarf Gourami* (C.lalia), the *Pearl* or *Lace Gourami* (Trichogaster leeri) and the *Moonlight Gourami* (T.microlepis).

Give us a kiss! The Kissing Gourami *(Helostoma temmincki)* uses its lips to rasp off algae from rocks, not to prove its affection for its owner

The Talking, or Croaking, Gourami *(Trichopsis pumilus),* makes audible sounds when courting

African species are also available but not to such a degree as the species described above. These fishes have the special labyrinth organ in their head which enable them to breathe atmospheric air.

The multi-coloured **Killifishes** from Africa and South America are the so-called 'annual' fishes described by Val on page 29. Aquarists throughout

A Killifish, also known as annual fish, whose eggs can be exchanged by post

the world take advantage of the ability of these fishes' eggs to withstand drying out, and exchange fertile fish eggs by post so that fishkeepers in other areas can have the pleasure of keeping these very beautiful fish — which often live much longer than one year in the aquarium where the water never dries up.

Killifishes do not need quite so high water temperatures as do the majority of tropical species — 65°-70°F is quite suitable, and in some centrally-heated rooms the aquarium heating system is often not required at all.

Whilst the Killifishes are normally found at the top of the water, **Catfishes** occupy the lowest layers. The *Corydoras* species (from South America) are amusing little characters, always scurrying around the aquarium floor apparently 'tidying up'. There is a specialist organisation which caters for aquarists who find these, and other catfishes, a stimulating challenge. Larger catfishes from Africa are very exotic looking with their characteristic development of barbels around the mouth.

The Armoured Catfish *(Callichthys callichthys)* is a bottom-dweller

Rasboras and **Danios** are colourful and very active fishes from India, Burma and the Far East. A favourite is the *Harlequin Fish* (Rasbora heteromorpha) easily recognised by the blue/black triangular marking on the sides of the body which is itself red and silver, so the fish is quite

Danio malebaricus, the Giant Danio, a fast-swimming, shoal-loving fish which will add speed and excitement to the aquarium

handsome. Other Rasboras may not be as striking in colours, but all may be considered lively additions to the tank. None grow too large, but some species appear to be more delicate than others and more demanding in their care.

Danios are fast, surface swimming, shoaling fishes and a well-known variety is the *Zebra Danio* (Brachydanio rerio) which has horizontal dark blue stripes on a gold or silver background. The *Leopard Danio* (Brachydanio frankei) has a spotted pattern and the *Pearl Danio* (Brachdanio albolineatus) is equally suitably named. Danios are very hardy and because they are easy breeders are likely to be inexpensive to buy.

Back on the bottom of the tank again, **Loaches** come in a wide choice of colour patterns, body shapes and sizes; the *Kuhli Loach* looks more like a

Spined Loaches are found in tropical and temperate areas; this is *Cobitis taenia,* a coldwater species

garden worm in a football jersey than a fish and is among the hardest fishes to net! **Botias** are sleek, pointed-nosed (complete with probing barbels) fishes, perhaps more nocturnal in their habits than most. The small *Chain Botia* (Botia sidthimunki) is very attractively marked, as is the much larger *Clown Loach* (B.macracantha) with its orange and black banded markings. In between these two sizes come many other colourful

Botia horae, the Skunk Loach, is a member of a large family of tropical loaches

specimens, and they all have a common characteristic — a sharp spine, in front of each eye, which they erect when threatened or perhaps netted; so be careful when transporting them.

In addition to these specimens briefly outlined there are many, many more that are available, but you will soon discover these for yourself as you go along. Most of the fish already described mix together in a community tank provided that you don't ask the impossible by expecting a large fish to ignore much tinier ones when it might be hungry! Remember, at the purchasing stage, all the fishes will be young specimens (with more growing to come) and we are talking about fishes in the 1½ inch to 2½ inch range. To save your turning back the pages; in our 'medium' tank of say, 2 ft long by 1 ft wide with a water surface area of 288 sq. inches, we can allow 36 'inches' of fishes. When buying fishes at the outset, do not buy the total allowable 'inches' as this will not give the fishes room to grow further; also remember that some species look better in a shoal, say six or more. It is almost unnecessary to advise against buying the most expensive fishes until you have mastered the basic art of keeping a few hardy specimens alive for some time.

Remaining with tropical fishes for a moment, the adventurous hobbyist may well progress on to the tropical *saltwater* varieties later on in his fishkeeping career — just another example of some of the fascinations that await.

Coldwater Fish

This section on fishes would be incomplete without reference to coldwater species, both native and imported. It is quite possible to keep the humble *Stickleback* and *Minnow* in an indoor aquarium. The former has an unusual spawning pattern, building a submerged nest of water plants in a tunnel form and laying the eggs inside. The Minnow may present a problem because it needs plenty of well aerated water and a powerful filtration system is one way of providing this.

Two fishes from our native streams: top, the Ten-Spined Stickleback *(Pygosteus pugnitius)*, and, bottom, the Minnow *(Phoxinus phoxinus)*

Everyone's idea of an aquarium fish — the Common Goldfish *(Carassius auratus)*

Most coldwater fishes come from the **Goldfish** group and they enjoy enthusiastic support from their devotees. One problem with coldwater fishes is that they are much larger than tropical species and correspondingly need larger living quarters. Many Fancy Goldfish are kept in outside ponds, only being brought indoors under cover during the frosty winter months. The appeal of these fishes is undoubtedly due to their colours, exotic body shapes and extended, exaggerated fins which have all been created by selective breeding over literally thousands of years.

Basic aquarium management techniques still apply, but perhaps undergravel filtration systems are unsuitable for the coldwater aquarium due to the foraging nature of the fishes which would soon render the system ineffectual.

In addition to the *Common Goldfish* (Carassius auratus), familiar to anyone who has ever tried to throw a table-tennis ball into a jam jar at a fair, more suitable fishes for the aquarium are the *Comet* and the *Shubunkin* varieties. The Comet has longer fins than the Common Goldfish, whilst the Shubunkin has multi-coloured scales of red, blue and black. These fishes have single tails whilst the next group, the *Fantail, Veiltail* and *Moor*, have divided tails and anal fins, their bodies are much shorter and the Moor might be the coldwater counterpart to the tropical Black Molly, as it is also jet black in colouration.

Thanks to genetic experimentation, more exotic body shapes and secondary growths around the head appear in the *Oranda, Lionhead* and *Pompon*; in the last two varieties the dorsal fin is absent. Again the anal and caudal fins are divided.

Face to face with Sir Goldfish. Males develop white pimples on the head and gill covers during breeding time

The final group of Fancy Goldfish includes the *Bubble-Eye* and the *Celestial* where the breeder's attention has resulted in the eye-structure becoming exaggerated with the eyes looking permanently upwards. No dorsal fins are present and again the anal and caudal fins are divided.

These are very advanced fishes indeed and such delicate fins and exotic shapes need correspondingly extra care to keep them in tip-top condition.

Another variation, apart from these physical characteristics, which adds extra interest is that the scales of these fishes may be any one of three types: metallic (i.e. shiny); nacreous (mother-of-pearl, semi-transparent); matt (no shine at all and the fish appears to be scaleless). You can see that although the number of varieties of coldwater fishes is limited, the true possibilities for the aquarist are very much larger.

85

Breeding

Perhaps the pinnacle of achievement for any aquarist is when his fishes breed in captivity. This may be a purely spontaneous, natural occurrence on the part of the fishes, or it may be the result of an encouragement, by the provision of ideal conditions, on the part of the aquarist. Whatever the reason, it must be taken as a sign that everything is highly satisfactory within the fishkeeper's tank.

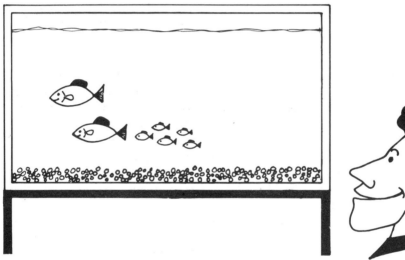

'A sign that everything is highly satisfactory . . .'

Sadly, many aquarists never know that some of their fishes have bred, nor even that some are capable of breeding, and only keep an aquarium as an extra decorative feature in the home. On the other hand, some hobbyists try to breed each and every fish they keep and it is through their continuing efforts that the hobby progresses, with the so-called 'difficult' fishes being bred increasingly in numbers. So, is it easy to reach this ultimate goal, or does it take years of experience?

The answer to these questions may be 'yes and no', or even 'no and yes', depending on what you want to do. Val has already found out that the livebearing fishes are easy to breed, but herein lies the difficulty: because they will interbreed so easily a close watch has to be kept to prevent unwanted breedings taking place. If the colour patterns, for instance, are to be maintained in a pure strain then other colour varieties of the same species of fish must not be introduced into the same tank as your intended breeding stock.

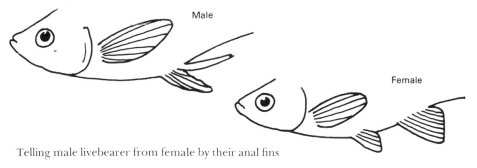

Telling male livebearer from female by their anal fins

Fortunately, the sexes are quite easy to differentiate, the males having a modified anal fin whilst that of the female fish is the normal fan shape. One of the fascinations of fish-breeding is the possibility for genetic experimentation, in the same way as gardeners used to strive for the 'black' tulip. You can imagine what can possibly be done with all the colour patterns by careful selective breeding programmes, so it is no wonder that the livebearing fishes are so popular. However, you must remember to plan well ahead (providing extra tank space, etc.), if you intend to follow this particular interest.

Let's go through a typical train of events of livebearing breeding. As you will soon discover, your female livebearer will lose no time in becoming gravid (pregnant) and you will notice her obviously getting fatter with a dark patch developing around the anal area. Sometimes, towards the end of her pregnancy you can see the babies' tiny eyes showing through the tightly stretched skin of the female's abdomen. If you let nature take its course the baby fishes will be born into the hazards of the community tank; some will find refuge in the plants, but these are the lucky ones. Others will be eaten by the other fishes in the tank. How can you help save the youngsters?

Well, remember that second, smaller tank you have got to act as a quarantine, or hospital, tank? That can now become a nursery! Female livebearers carry their young for about a month, and you will soon become adept at gauging the state of the pregnancy by watching carefully.

A suddenly thin female indicates a recent 'happy event' has occurred, and a month from now she will probably be ready to drop another batch of babies. Now is the time to prepare that second tank with plenty of bushy plants (and a heater and thermostat!) and as soon as the female begins to fatten out put her into this new home. Don't wait until nearly a month is up as the shock of moving a highly gravid fish will cause premature birth and the young fishes may not survive.

When the births occur, some aquarists allow the female a day or two's rest before returning her to the hustle and bustle of the community tank

Separate the gravid mother and her first fry from the main tank

where she will soon attract the amorous attentions of the males once more. In addition to the separate nursery tank, there are plastic 'breeding traps' — small tanks with internal divisions which separate Mum from her new-born children. These traps may be hung in the main aquarium, but many pregnant fishes are frightened by being so confined, so if you can provide a separate maternity tank so much the better.

Baby livebearers are able to take normal foods straightaway, although flake foods may need to be crumbled between the fingers first. Brine shrimp, newly-hatched, is excellent too.

Although you have managed to save a lot of tiny fishes from being eaten by other fishes, not all of them will be 'up to standard'; some may have wrong markings, some may not grow as fast as the others, and some may, unfortunately, be deformed. It is best to get rid of these unwanted youngsters as soon as possible, and they may be fed to your other fishes as live food; only keep the best of the youngsters to continue the strain. I know this sounds heartless, having gone to all that trouble to save them in the first place, but as in nature, it is the survival of the fittest, i.e. the best, that we are after. If you keep every single youngster that is presented to you, you will soon run out of tank space! Another consideration is that any unwanted youngster also consumes food and time to look after it.

After this run-down of the problems of livebearing fishes you may be forgiven for thinking that easily bred fishes are not always the perfect answer!

The egglaying fishes do not necessarily provide the ideal answer either, as they have their own sets of problems to be overcome but, luckily, they provide their own rewards.

The first problem for the would-be breeder is to be able to pick out a male and female fish from which to attempt to breed! Unlike the livebearing fishes they do not have easy guides to their sexes but a general rule of thumb is that male fishes are usually more brightly coloured, have more elongated fins and are of slimmer build.

The next problem is to get the fishes into the right frame of mind to breed, a process which is called 'conditioning'. Again we can make use of that second tank but this time we must know how the fishes actually breed before we furnish it — are they egg-scatterers, bubble-nest builders; do they guard their eggs and young? A tank furnished with rocky caves and flower pots will do nicely for egg-hiding cichlids but is useless for egg-scattering barbs or tetras. Some bubble-nest builders need some plant material in their nest construction or a small piece of floating polystyrene will do to anchor the bubbles. In addition to these practical considerations, the fishes should *want* to breed and may depend on you the aquarist to some extent to persuade them. 'Absence makes the heart grow fonder' is as true for fishes as it is for humans, so it is normal practice for the male and female fishes to be kept apart from each other for a couple of weeks before you let them breed. This 'conditioning' can take place in the second tank; it can have a glass partition across it to separate 'him' from 'her', and seems to be extra effective by virtue of the fact that while the fish can see each other, they cannot reach each other! (We aquarists are a heartless lot really, aren't we!)

During this separation period each fish should be given the very best of foods, particularly live foods if at all possible. Come the big day when the partition is removed (you may arrange to do this at weekends when you

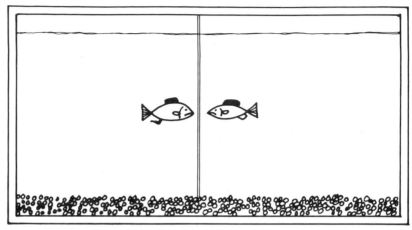

'Absence makes the heart grow fonder . . . we aquarists are a heartless lot, aren't we!'

have time to watch what happens) and the fish are reunited! The male, after some arrogant showing off in front of the female, generally drives her into the bushy plants, or nylon wool mops, where the eggs are scattered and fertilised. The parents are best removed after spawning activity ceases, perhaps after an hour or so.

Your aquatic books will give approximate times for hatching; but after a day or so, tiny 'splinters' may be seen hanging on the glass, and soon these become tiny specks darting around the tank. Because of their smaller size, the fry of egglaying fishes need smaller first foods than do the livebearer babies. There are liquid fry foods on the market suitable for them, and a favourite standby of aquarists is a piece of hard-boiled egg yolk wrapped in a piece of cloth squeezed in the water of their tank. The young fish will feed on the yellow suspension in the water, but be careful not to overdo the feeding! Cultures of *infusoria* can also be made: usually the recipe is for some form of vegetable material to be allowed to rot in water (lettuce leaves, banana skins, potato peel, dried grass cuttings, etc.), and the micro-organisms which develop in the water provide the fish with a tiny living first food. Infusoria is cultured in jam jars stood in a sunny spot, but beware of the smell — a kitchen window spot is not always appreciated by the rest of the family!

Soon, however, the young fry can be fed on larger foods, the brine shrimp diet may be introduced and the fry rapidly put on size and weight.

A variation on the theme of bushy plants to protect the eggs from hungry parents is two or three layers of glass marbles on the tank floor.

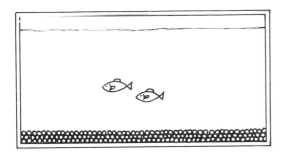

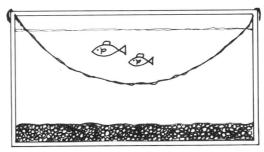

Protecting the eggs from hungry parents

The eggs fall between the crevices and the parent fish cannot get at them to eat them. Some egg-scattering fishes may be spawned as a shoal, and here all the males are conditioned together in one tank while the females are prepared likewise in another. Sometimes netting is laid in the spawning tank and all the pairs of fishes put into the tank above the net so that all the eggs from the mass spawning fall through the net to safety in the hatching tank below. Zebra Danios may be bred in this manner, and one further advantage of this system is that it's easy to catch all the fish afterwards — just lift out the net!

Fishes that exercise parental care, i.e. Cichlids, Gouramies (nest-builders) and mouthbrooders, usually pick their own breeding partners through a process of natural selection (we humans call it love!). They then clear a spawning site, or the male blows a bubble-nest, eggs are laid and fertilised and then one, or both, of the parent fishes look after the eggs and subsequent young. Sometimes one parent is driven off after spawning and if this occurs it is best to remove the persecuted fish for its own sake. Depending on the size of the young, similar arrangements for feeding apply as for the young of the egg-scattering species.

Apart from the mouthbrooders, eggs may be taken away from the parents and raised separately in another tank if required, but it is much better to let nature take its course — then you can have the pleasure of watching a fish family in the making, all of your own.

Among the egglaying fishes, the Zebra Danio and the Rosy Barb are two of the easiest to spawn and can be recommended as a beginner's choice. The Thicklip, and the Three-Spot Gouramies are also easy spawners; I have had success with the Dwarf Gourami too, but the fry are so small that a very small first food has to be found for them and this may be problematical for the novice.

Some of the dwarf cichlids (Apistogramma species) are relatively simple spawners, although they are so secretive about it that you don't always see what goes on until Mum brings out her youngsters from a cave for their first airing. The larger cichlid, the Blue Acara (Aequidens pulcher) is also a favourite breeder but tends to be a bit aggressive towards other fishes, particularly tempting-looking Neon Tetras! Larger cichlids may also uproot plants in their pre-spawning courtship so it is best to give them a robustly furnished tank to themselves from the word go, and let them get on with it!

The challenges thrown up in fishbreeding are fascinating; whilst some aquarists struggle on for years trying to breed something (like me and my Angelfish!), others seem blessed with a 'wet thumb' (the fishkeeper's equivalent to the gardener's 'green fingers') and practically spawn fish almost at will — doesn't it make you sick!

Coldwater fishbreeding, which in nature physically follows the normal egg-scattering pattern, brings its own refinement to the hobby. Practised over literally thousands of years by aquarists it is perhaps only natural that it has become the most sophisticated. Remember, the goldfish (and all its variations) has been aquarium raised specifically for its physical beauty, colours and finnage development; fishes selected for parenthood are chosen because they possess all the qualities that the breeder is looking for, but which might not be present in any one fish (colour and size in one, finnage development or body shape in another). Such fishes are bred together and their offspring further re-mated to produce that hoped-for perfect fish.

Coldwater breeding programmes have become so advanced that young fishes are produced without their parents ever meeting! (I suppose that makes them all fish orphans?) The female is selected when full of eggs, which are then 'stripped' from her by hand into a shallow bowl of water. The male (recognised at breeding time by the white tubercules, or pimples, which he develops on his gill covers) is then similarly manually 'milked' of his fertilising fluid into the same bowl. The contents are then stirred, so that the eggs become fertilised. The eggs are allowed to hatch naturally, and the young fish reared, and quality selected, in the usual way. You must appreciate that this is the method used in commercial hatcheries who do not want unsaleable, unwanted spawnings to occur, only requiring the best youngsters from the best parents.

Faced with all these possibilities and methods of spawning, the newcomer to the hobby should have no difficulty in finding one family of fishes likely to suit his needs and very soon will start hearing the patter of tiny fins!

Books and Societies

It is very difficult for the experienced to know just how much information to give to the novice: too much, and it is 'off-putting'; too little, and there's no confidence to start! Talking to Val and, through this book, to you makes me realise how much knowledge one gathers over the years, and to how much the newcomer has to look forward. I believe that the best thing to say in conclusion is, 'Yes. I'd do it all over again' — I don't think I'll ever stop learning about the wonderful world of fishes. Good fishkeeping!

Books

KTG Aquaria by Dick Mills (EP Publishing, 1978).
Dictionary of Proper and Common Names of Freshwater Fishes (Fed. of British Aquatic Societies, 1976).
Scientific Names and their Meanings (Fed. of British Aquatics Societies, 1977).
National Show Fish Sizes (Fed. of British Aquatic Societies, 1973 *et. seq.*).
Aquarium Technology by A. Jenno (Barry Shurlock, 1976).
How Fishes Live by P. Whitehead (Elsevier-Phaidon, 1975).
The Complete Aquarium Encyclopedia of Tropical Freshwater Fish by J. D. von Ramshorst (Elsevier-Phaidon, 1978).
Freshwater Fishes of the World by G. Sterba (Studio Vista, 1966; TFH, 1973).

Periodicals

Aquarist and Pondkeeper. The Butts, Half Acre, Brentford, Middlesex.
Practical Fishkeeping: EMAP National Publications Ltd., Bretton Court, Bretton, Peterborough.
Tropical Fish Hobbyist: 13 Nutley Lane, Reigate, Surrey.
Freshwater and Marine Aquarium: 120 W. Sierra Madre Blvd., PO Box 487, Sierra Madre, California 91024, USA.

Useful Addresses

Federation of British Aquatic Societies: General Secretary, Hugh Parrish, 18 The Barons, St. Margarets, Twickenham, Middlesex.
Federation of Northern Aquarium Societies: Secretary, A. Darby, 1 Perrin Street, Hyde, Cheshire.
Federation of Scottish Aquatic Societies: Secretary, R. A. Dunleavy, 13 Dryburgh Street, Whitehill, Hamilton, Scotland.

Printed and bound in Great Britain at The Pitman Press, Bath